JoAnn ScrapEssentials

IDEA BOOK

for scrapbooking and paper crafts

NANC & CO.

acknowledgements

JoAnn ScrapEssential Idea Book for Scrapbooking and Paper Crafts Volume 2 was written by NanC and Company and published by Leisure Arts, Inc.

Author: Nancy M. Hill

Senior Design Director: Nancy M. Hill

Senior Editor: Shannon Ogden

Senior Graphic Designer: Rafael Nielson

Assistant Graphic Designers: Tai Anderson, Lynn Walker, Trevor Howard, Teresa Hansen, Julie Walker, Danelle Larsen, Guy Wymore

Cover Designers: Rafael Neilson, Tai Anderson

Photographers: Daniel Parker Smith, Shannon Ogden, Rafael Nielson

Writers: Jeanne Taylor, Candice Smoot, Shannon Ogden

Copy Editors: Miles Ogden, Betty Henderson, Donna Hill, Erin Madsen

NanC & Company Designers: Shannon Ogden, Erin Madsen, Vanessa Braswell, Kristine McKay, Jeanne Taylor

For information about sales visit the Memories in the Making web site at **www.leisurearts.com**

author's letter

Scrapbooking and Card Making have Blossomed into a Whirlwind of Craft Projects

Our dedicated designers and staff at NanC and Company are delighted to bring you this 2nd Volume of the *JoAnn Scrap Essentials Idea Book*. We have had so much fun taking scrapbooking and cardmaking a step further into paper crafting and focusing on gifts, albums, party and holiday projects, home décor, journaling and other creative techniques.

From incredible scrapbook pages and unique cards to paper covered boxes or grandma brag wallets, you are sure to find many paper craft ideas that use the great variety of products found in the JoAnn stores. When you see the JoAnn Scrap Essentials' logo you will know that the project showcased includes a JoAnn Essentials' item. This is the special JoAnn product that cannot be found anywhere else.

Our Senior Editor, Shannon Ogden, and our Senior Graphic Artist, Rafael Nielson, have been incredibly creative in helping to make sure this publication includes a wide variety of projects for beginning to advanced crafters.

Idea "lifting" (aka stealing) is perfectly acceptable! In fact, we expect that this Idea Book will save you time and energy. Most of us have far more photos and creative energy than we have ideas–so take the great designs and projects shown on these pages and make them your own.

We wish you happy scrapping and paper crafting!

Nancy

Nancy M. Hill of NanC and Company
President/Founder DieCuts With a View

table of contents

BUDDY
PAL
AMIGO
friend

outdoor
easy
FUN

HONEYMOON
DUCKMOBILE TOUR

P
love

Articles

fresh ideas for scrapbooking and crafting

We believe you want more from your scrapbooking. You seek to express new levels of creativity and personal style not only just in your scrapbooks but all around your home. You love to invent new scrapbooking techniques. We understand the way you think. We know you want to go beyond traditional scrapbooking techniques and products. You want more. You want to create scrapbook and papercrafting treasures from uncommon sources. You want your scrapbooks and your home to stand out from the crowd and to reveal your own unique style and flare for life.

We challenge you to think outside the box. It is possible to do with some effort and practice. Revamp your scrapbooking with unexpected items and transform the craft store offerings into a world of embellishments with scrapbooking tools, techniques and products. We hope the following ideas inspire you to think in new ways and to create projects with a new level of creativity.

scrapbooking

Forgotten odds and ends found at home, in the mail, at a flea market, hardware store or all over the craft store often add the most flavor to scrapbook pages. Using what you already have on hand or purchasing discounted items lets your scrapbooking budget stretch further, allowing you to create even more pages or to splurge on those items you can't live without. Find new and treasured uses for those items collecting dust in the attic.

give forgotten objects a second chance

Rejuvenate children's board books by painting the pages to create a fresh start for a mini or gift album. Refinish old photo albums by touching up or recovering covers and filling the insides with archival safe paper and cardstock. Even matchbooks and mailed compact disc tins can creatively house scrapbook pages once given a little bit of paint and paper.

Fill scrapbooks with meaningful items such as old stationery, favorite prints or ads no longer being used. Salvage old cross-stitch crafts from old frames or pillows for use in a cherished scrapbook.

let hobbies do double duty

Use remnants from other projects and hobbies such as fabric, lace, ribbon, wire and thread to add character to your pages. A sewing machine's decorative stitches add subtle detail that give the perfect finishing touch to a page. Jewelry-making supplies such as beads and charms are ideal for scrapbooking. Glue beads to paper or string them to create a frame around a photo. Attach charms to tags with a brad. Even leftover hardware can be a great addition to a scrapbook page.

inspiration is all around you

Take a walk outside for inspiration. Gather scrapbooking supplies such as leaves, flowers and bark. To add the right mood to a page, try arranging pressed plants onto your scrapbook page.

Take notice of items that please you. The label from a bottled beverage or a collection of bottle caps might be the perfect way to accent a photo. Inspiration is all around if you are open to new possibilities.

Search your home, yard sales, thrift stores, nature and craft stores for supplies to create varied and meaningful pages for your scrapbooks. Always remember to use archival-safe products when possible so your pages can be preserved for years to come.

crafting

Think outside scrapbooking. Why let your unique creativity stop there? Get out your scrapbooking supplies and let your mind take flight. Countless projects around the home can be completed using products you already have on hand and techniques you have already mastered. So look around your home; it's time to finish those projects you've been thinking about for years and give your home a fresh, new look.

home décor

Wall Art

Have you ever walked into a home with a variety of decorations on the walls? They beckon you in and captivate your interest. Liven up your walls with plates, needle work, mirrors, artwork, pictures, wall hangings, sconces, magnetic boards and more. With a little effort, simple scrapbooking techniques can add a fresh look to any of these objects. Try creating faux picture frames from cardstock with mitered corners or embellishing purchased frames with your choice of scrapbooking supplies. Paint, decoupage or adorn frames with rub-ons for a new twist or embellish the frame of a mirror with tiles to create a mosaic of color.

Frame mirrors, chalk boards, cork boards, magnetic boards or a creation of your own. Create a collage of your favorite sayings, words, photographs and drawings. Make a padded display board with batting, fabric, ribbon and push pins. Fill a frame with your favorite scrapbook page for display. Mat a photograph with ribbon; title it using a metal bookplate.

Furniture

Alter furniture with scrapbooking supplies and techniques. Decoupage a chair or table top with a favorite collection of paper and images. Crackle paint, decoratively paint or stencil a piece of furniture that needs a makeover. Try using brads as faux upholstery nails to give an upholstered foot stool old world charm.

decorative odds and ends

Decoupage

For a sophisticated look, decoupage the glass container of a candle with a favorite paper, photograph or other image. When the candle is lit, a glow will illuminate your chosen paper or image. Decorate the candle with ribbon and metal frames for embellishment. Decoupage can personalize the look of any item, including: coasters, chargers, clocks, chairs, trays and even vases.

Wooden Blocks

Make ordinary blocks of wood come alive with paint, rub-ons, decoupage and stickers. Attach a word that will make you happy each time you see it or make children's building blocks match your chosen color palette.

kids will be kids

Locker and School Art

Give the inside of your locker a refreshing break with bright colors and inspiring words. Attach magnets to the back of metal and acrylic words for a pick me up every time you go to your locker. Attach the magnetic embellishments to the inside of the locker door and use them to display photographs, notes or favorite poems. Hang a bag of potpourri you've embellished to make your locker smell great. Cover school and music books with favorite papers, words, bubbles and other embellishments to personalize and protect your work books.

Children's Room Decorations

Create door curtains with rows of ribbons, buttons and beads. Embellish the ribbons with eyelets, ribbon charms, beads, buttons and word pins making sure to weight the bottoms of the ribbons so they will hang properly in the door frame. Your daughter will remember you every time she leaves or enters her room.

Attach large eyelets to the top of curtains, thread with ribbon and tie to a curtain rod. Create pull-backs for the curtains by attaching large eyelets to opposite sides of a rectangular piece of fabric. Pull the curtains back with the rectangular piece of fabric and place the eyelets onto a hook attached to the wall beside the window. Add beads, charms and embellishments down the vertical seams or along the bottoms of roman shades for more playful window decorations. Sew pockets into window or bed curtains made of sheer fabric and fill with flowers, notes, charms and more.

Decorate wooden letters to spell out a child's name or initials and display on a book shelf, hang from pegs with ribbon or attach to a wall. Create faux stained glass with colorful vellum tags tied into the shape of a star or heart and hang from a window with fishing line.

Toys

Create a child's activity mat for hours of entertainment and fun. Cut blocks from fabric and create an activity on each block. Sew a ribbon with a button to one side of a block and sew a button hole on the other side of the block and teach your child to use buttons. Attach four or more eyelets to another square and thread with a shoelace to teach your child how to lace shoes and tie bows. Sew all blocks together, finish off the edges and make sure everything is secure so as not to pose a choking hazard. Adorn ordinary quilts with scrapbooking supplies, such as buttons! Use buttons and eyelets as decorative touches to flowers or pewter words on a jean quilt.

Create a puzzle from a collage of papers, images, stickers and rub-ons. Decoupage the collage and cut into puzzle pieces with an exacto knife or scissors. Create a tic-tac-toe board with a decorated cardboard base and charms as the x's and o's. Experiment with your child's favorite game or invent a new one of your own.

celebrate good times

Decorations

Nothing is as fun as decorating your home for a festive gathering, be it Christmas, Hanukkah, a birthday or anniversary. Decorate the back of dining room or kitchen chairs by attaching a bouquet of flowers to the back of a chair with ribbon. Create place settings by turning wire into mini photo holders and placing an old picture of each guest in the wire holders. This will not only let guests know where to sit but will also spark a fun conversation. Create cardstock place settings that match the theme of the party and the invitations.

Costumes

Create festive costumes with paper and scrapbooking supplies. For example, create birthday hats by rolling patterned paper into a cone, attaching two eyelets at opposite sides of the base of the hat and threading ribbon through each eyelet to be tied together under the chin. Many Halloween costumes can be made with wire, paper and cardstock. For example, create a bird's wings from wire covered with mulberry paper; cut a beak and ears out of cardstock. Paint wooden shoes with green shamrocks for St. Patrick's Day or pink-and-red hearts for Valentine's Day.

give the perfect gift

There is nothing quite like giving a homemade present to someone special. The time and effort you put into making the gift shows just how much you care. Your scrapbooking expertise will come in handy when making and wrapping these special gifts.

Homemade Gifts

Mark a favorite excerpt from a cherished book with a personalized bookmark as a gift for a book club friend. Choose an initial and give a letter silver clip as the personalized bookmark. Create necklaces and bracelets of any style with a variety of scrapbooking beads and charms available. Make ribbon belts by stitching belt loops or a belt buckle to one side of a ribbon. If using a belt buckle, attach eyelets to the opposite side of the ribbon, like belt holes, making sure the eyelets are large enough for the buckle to fit through.

Wrapping

Finish off a homemade gift with wrapping paper you have made yourself. Create a bag from patterned paper and cardstock, decorate a pre-made bag or use patterned paper as wrapping paper. Make a card to match the gift wrap and finish off with filling made from old scrapbooking paper that has been crimped and put through a shredder.

express yourself

We hope that this collection of ideas will help you put to use the many crafting supplies found at JoAnn Fabric store. Look at scrapbooking supplies in diverse and clever ways. You will find inspiration for scrapbook pages in unexpected places and objects. Remember, this is just the beginning. Get together with friends and let these ideas spark new creations and worlds within the walls of your very own homes.

special
GRANDMOMMY'S
BRAG book

Chapter 1

gift ideas

Close your eyes and imagine the excitement in your best friend's eyes as she unwraps your surprise gift; it's just what she's always wanted. We all love gifts, both giving and receiving. Gift giving celebrates life and love. Let the ideas in this chapter inspire your mind to create gifts you can give the person "who has everything" or for the person whom you would do anything. Give your gifts a personal touch that only you can give.

gift ideas

Jo-Ann ScrapEssentials

grandpa's adventure box

Designer: NanC & Company

Cover the card box with patterned paper and distress with ink. Add letters, wire wrapped matches and fishing lure. Stitch pre-made cards together to create an album. Cover the album with assorted letters, tied ribbons and embellishments. Sand and ink the papers and staple on ribbons. Put the album inside the box.

Jo-Ann ScrapEssentials

party girl clipboard

Designer: Anna Nielson

Cover a clip board with patterned paper. Embellish with adhesive ribbon, fibers, acrylic word, metal tag, photo turns and rub-ons. Ink and add a vellum envelope and flower diecuts.

angie's address book

Designer: Susan Stringfellow

Jo-Ann ScrapEssentials

Cover address book with patterned paper. Embellish with 3-D appliqué stickers, paper flowers, brads, bookplate and a ribbon bow. Add metal letters to inside cardstock tabs. Stamp tile page and attach ribbon with brad.

Jo-Ann ScrapEssentials

sunburn first aid kit

Designer: Sam Cousins

Embellish a ready-made first aid kit. Decoupage patterned paper, wave diecut and transparency title to container. Finish with fiber, charm and bottle cap.

gift ideas

daisy luggage tag

Designer: Caroline Lau

Create a cardstock tag; embellish with cardstock flowers and tuck inside a luggage tag. Embellish the hanger with tied ribbons.

Jo-Ann ScrapEssentials

grandmommy's brag book

Designer: Lily Goldsmith

Decoupage a wallet with patterned paper. Embellish with ribbon, quote, 3-D letters and a charm. Cut tags and attach photos; insert into credit card holder.

JoAnn ScrapEssentials

through the years

Designer: Anna Estrada Davidson

Create an accordion pocket booklet. Adhere assorted stickers, rub-on and vellum quotes. Embellish with ribbon, flower, brad and tag.

step 1

Adhere cardstock band to background to create pocket; ink the edges. Cut tag and adhere vellum quote with brads. Tie ribbon knot to top of the tag.

step 2

Journal inside pocket album with rubber stamps, handwriting and rub on letters. Embellish with stickers, brads and flower.

step 3

Embellish the cover with a circle photo matted on patterned paper, chipboard letter, ribbon knot and charm. Add sticker flower and tie closed with ribbon.

Jo-Ann ScrapEssentials

apple recipe box

Designer: Susan Stringfellow

Decoupage patterned paper on a wood recipe box. Cut out paper apples and adhere to chipboard. Stamp title and place under painted bookplate with ribbon knots. Adhere pom-pom fringe to the front of box. Make coordinating recipe cards to fill inside.

Jo-Ann ScrapEssentials

notes for miss massey

Designer: Sam Cousins

Alter a wood sign; paint and cover with sanded cardstock and rub-on letters. Add 3-D stickers, metal clip and ribbons.

true friends

Designer: NanC & Company

Jo-Ann ScrapEssentials

Fold cardstock to create a tag album. Cover with patterned paper and rub-on quotes. Add ribbon, fiber, tags, metals and 3-D embellishments. Tie closed with a rubber band.

inspirational tag book

Designer: Maria Burke

Create a tag book. Cover several tags with cardstock and patterned paper. Fill tags with quotes, 3-D embellishments and connect with a metal chain.

gift ideas

JoAnn ScrapEssentials

flower coaster set

Designer: Jessica Ulery

Diecut flowers out of cardstock; stitch on circle centers. Stack coasters and tie with ribbon. Add metal bookplate with a safety pin. Fill bookplate with handwritten title.

dad glass frame

Designer: NanC & Company

Use a sanded overlay to mat a special drawing and title. Display inside a glass block frame.

coasters

Do you want to give creative gifts to people who have everything? Coasters are practical and original gifts that you can give to anyone. They can be made from plexi-glass, cardstock, cardboard or wood. You can decorate coasters with a variety of materials such as metals, stickers, patterned paper, rub-ons, dried flowers and pictures. If you want to make the coasters waterproof, add several layers of decoupage or laminate. There are a several ways to display coasters besides stacking them on the coffee table. You can string ribbon through plexi-glass coasters and hang them as artwork. You could also attach metal hangers to the backs of coordinating coasters with nails and arrange them on the wall. When creating coasters for gifts make the project meaningful to the recipient: color coordinate the coasters with the person's house, use their favorite color, or make coasters that reflect the person's personality or interests. Use your imagination to create wonderful works of art and gifts of love.

JoAnn ScrapEssentials

plexi-glass coaster

Designer: NanC & Company

Fill an acrylic frame with patterned paper, matted photo, stickers and stapled adhesive ribbon.

gift ideas

Jo-Ann ScrapEssentials

mini file folder album

Designer: Alecia Ackerman Grimm

Embellish a file folder with patterned paper, stickers, quote and 3-D embellishments. Attach photo sleeves to the file folder. Fill with mini scrapbook pages, journaling and embellishments. Fasten closed with a paper clip.

Jo-Ann ScrapEssentials

my teacher thank you gift

Designer: Cindy Smith

Cut patterned paper background and ink edges. Attach sticker with foam tape adhesive. Tie fabric strips around lid, add metal tag and metal accent.

family birthdays album

Designer: Sarah Adams

Cover album with patterned paper and inked cardstock. Create title with rub-on letters, cardstock and tag. Tie ribbon knots down spine of album.

altered apple recipe tin

Designer: Heather Seibel

Cover a metal lunch box with decoupaged patterned paper, chip board letters and rub-on letters. Attach assorted ribbons and bead tassel to outside of box. Fill inside with embellished recipe cards.

gift ideas

birthday bag

Designer: NanC & Company

Adhere cardstock and patterned paper to gift bag. Embellish with a tag and a stitched pocket. Tie ribbon knots on handle.

monogram birthday invitation

Designer: NanC & Company

Cut and round patterned paper and cardstock blocks. Ink and sand the edges. Embellish with ribbon knots and a matted monogram.

step 1

Cut out large cardstock circle. Using the diagram below, cut and fold the cardstock into a purse. Attach an eyelet to each corner. Cut two small rings out of cardstock. Fold small rings in half and adhere sides together to make two small semi-circles.

step 2

Fold the large circle into a purse and adhere in place. To make handles, place eyelets on the corners of the semi-circles and attach to the purse with twisted wire.

step 3

Embellish with patterned paper and cardstock. Hold purse closed with a brad and latch.

pink purse

Designer: Julie McGuffie, Scrapbook Memories Host

Fold and create purse from patterned cardstock and patterned paper. Attach handles with eyelets and wire. Attach metal closure on front and add patterned cardstock cutouts.

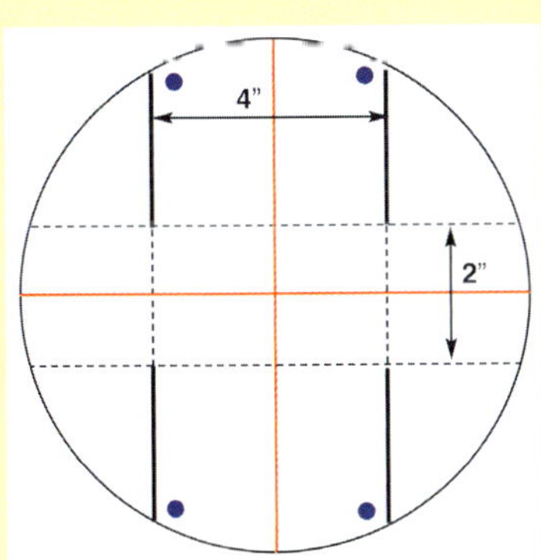

kelly
together
laugh
sweet

Chapter 2

albums

While pouring through the pages of cherished scrapbook albums, your mind can not help but bring back poignant memories of friends and loved ones allowing you to relive moments simple and great. Create albums as personal histories to document trips, preserve heritage and share with others. This section contains sample pages so you can see how other artists carry stylistic themes throughout their albums. Notice how colors coordinate and embellishments repeat to create harmony throughout an album.

albums

boy mini album

Designer: Carolyn Lontin

JoAnn ScrapEssentials

Tie small pieces of ribbon on the spine of a small pre-made album. Staple ribbon loops to tab the pages. Decorate the cover with patterned paper, flowers and clip; create title with rub-on quote. On the inside pages, handwrite and rubber stamp journaling. Use rub-on quotes and letters to title the photos. Finish with aging ink and mini flowers with colorful brad centers.

portland trip album

Designer: Carrie Gay

Attach ribbon loops to edge of pages. Cover inside with patterned paper, stickers, 3-D letters, stapled ribbons, flower and brads. Embellish cover with flower, tags, stamped image and initial.

albums

Jo-Ann ScrapEssentials

a new start... life in rescue

Designer: Cheryl Baase

Cut two pieces of chipboard, cover with patterned paper and bind with ring clips. Tie fabric strips along spine, ink and sand the edges. Create title with rub-ons. Create hidden journaling under a hinged photo. Cover inside pages with patterned paper, pockets, tags, rub-ons, ribbon and assorted embellishments.

JoAnn ScrapEssentials

senior pictures album

Designer: Sue Fields

Create a library pocket album with patterned paper and cardstock. Embellish cover with ribbon metal charm, wood numbers and epoxy sticker. Fill the inside pockets with ribbon-topped tags and assorted paper clips. Journal the tags with stickers, stamping and handwritten notes.

JoAnn ScrapEssentials

altered purse accordion album

Designer: Amy Smith

Create an accordion gift album inside a purse. Embellish with patterned paper, quotes and stickers. Enclose the album in purse and tie with ribbon. Create a coordinating cardstock card and tie with ribbon on opposite side.

home circle journal

Designer: Carolyn Lontin

Cover a spiral journal with patterned paper, ribbon and metal buckle. Cover inside pages with patterned paper, ribbons, paint chips and assorted 3-D metal embellishments. Print journaling on cardstock and attach with spiral clips, safety pins and brads.

Jo-Ann ScrapEssentials

my summer trip album

Designer: Heather Siebel

Create an album with a road map. Cover the front with a stamped title and epoxy stickers. On the map, attach photos, stamped and hand-written journaling and 3-D embellishments. Fold closed and tie with ribbon.

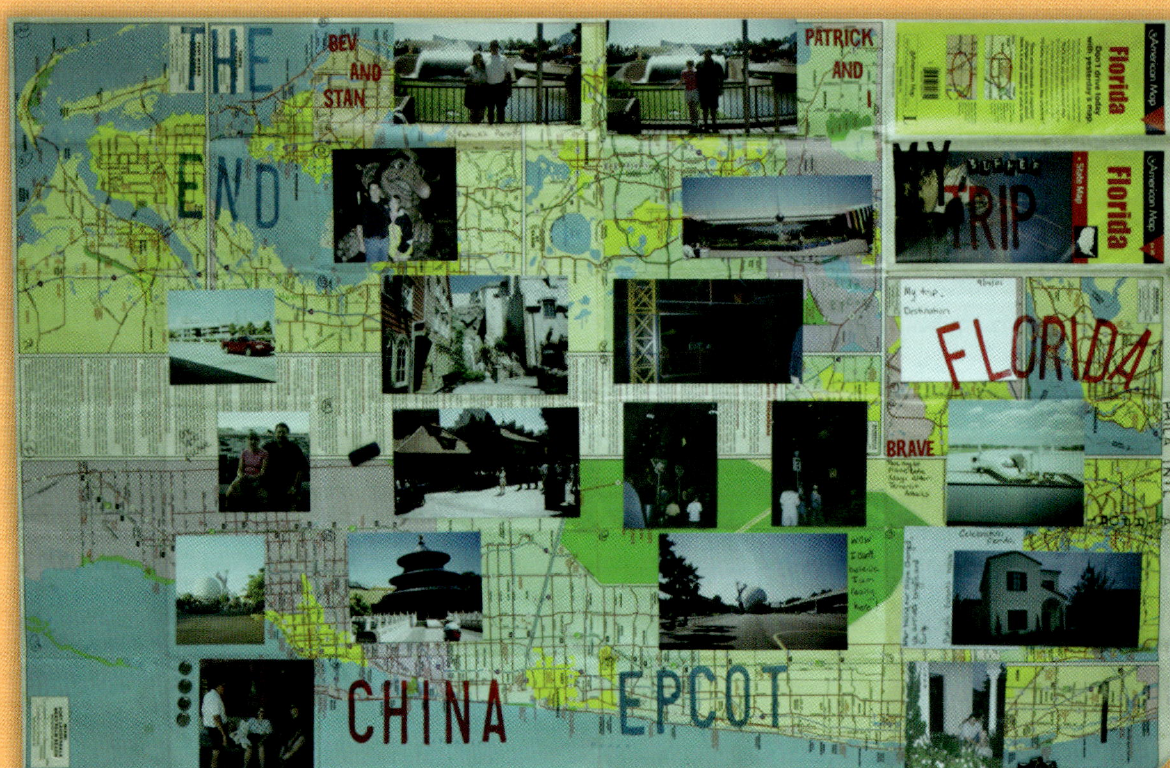

lake ontario paper bag album

Designer: Marcy Mahar

Create a paper bag album with a bag and patterned paper; cut the pages in lengths to give a stepped effect. Embellish the cover with stickers, ribbon and metal bookplate. Cover the inside pages with photos; journal with rub-on letters, stickers and handwriting.

Jo-Ann ScrapEssentials

bailey's book

Designer: NanC & Company

Embellish the cover of a pre-made album with patterned paper, adhesive ribbon, monogram letter and bookplate. Cover inside pages with patterned paper, metals, stickers and 3-D embellishments. Finish with children's handwriting and pictures.

weight loss diary

Designer: Mandy McQuillis

Cover album with cardstock, mesh and patterned paper. Paint and sand chipboard letter. Create title with rub-on and labeler stickers. Embellish with ribbon and silk flower. Fill inside pages with patterned paper, rub-ons, ribbons, assorted embellishments and printed journaling.

albums

JoAnn ScrapEssentials

my trip to disneyland accordion album

Designer: NanC & Company

Create a paint chip accordion album. Use over-sized paint chip cards to create pages for album. Create background with patterned-paper mosaic squares; staple assorted patterned-paper strips. Ink and sand the edges. Personalize with a hidden journaling tag, 3-D embellishments, stickers, ribbon and brads.

nana's brag book

Designer: NanC & Company

Jo-Ann ScrapEssentials

Sew paper bags together to create an album. Embellish cover with patterned paper and cardstock. Create the title with cork and rub-on letters. Fill inside with patterned paper, cardstock, tabs and 3-D embellishments. Create journaling tags that can pull out of the pockets.

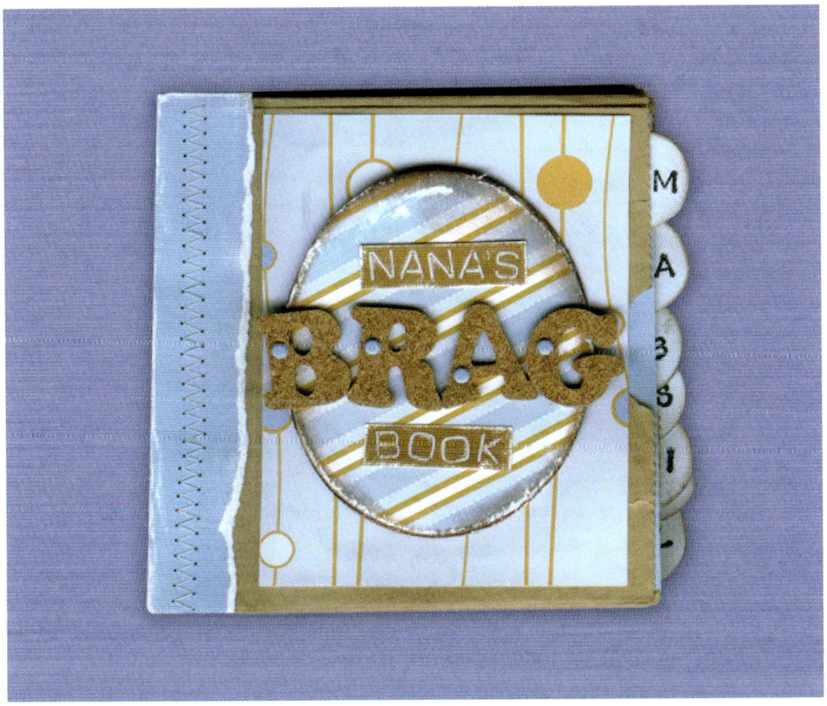

photo shoot album

Designer: Janet Schroeder

Personalize the cover with rub-on letters and a metal charm. Cover inside album with patterned paper, cardstock and photos. Add ribbons, quotes, stickers and 3-D embellishments.

family score book

Designer: Alecia Ackerman Grimm

Cover journal with patterned paper and 3-D embellishments. Create the title with letter stickers. Create inside page tabs with game score cards, patterned paper and 3-D stickers. Fill pages with personalized journaling, photos, rub-ons and embellishments.

albums

childhood memories album

Designer: Alecia Ackerman Grimm

Distress an album cover and cardstock frame with ink. Adhere frame and fill with an assortment of objects. Use diamond glaze adhesive to hold in place. Create inside pages with distressed cardstock, patterned paper and ribbon. Embellish with brads, flowers, metal charms and rhinestones.

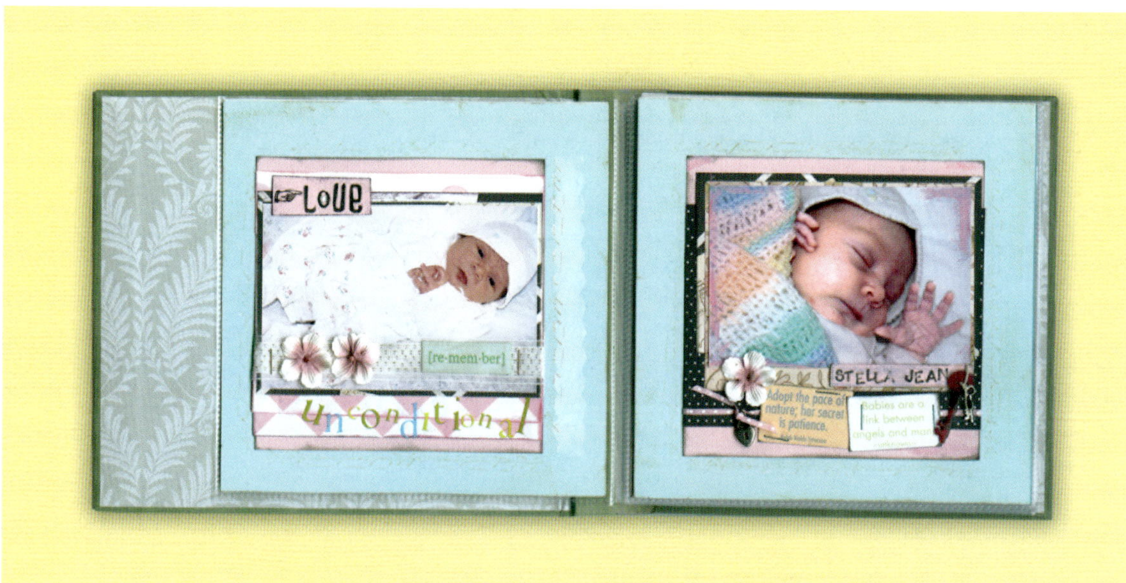

JoAnn ScrapEssentials

july vacation matchbook album

Designer: Leisure Arts

Create a tiny accordion album to fit inside a matchbox sleeve. Embellish with photos and journaling. Attach stamped metal tag to the matchbook. Hold closed with elastic band and hook-and-eye closures.

JoAnn ScrapEssentials

cousins paintchip mini album

Designer: NanC & Company

Create a special mini album with oversized paint chips. Embellish cover with rub-ons, matted stickers and bookplates. Fill inside pages with unique quotes, stickers, ribbon knots and photo turns. Use assorted ribbon for binding and for a closing tie.

love album

Designer: Maria Burke

Embellish the cover of a pre-made fabric album with stitched patterned paper and letters. Create the inside pages with cardstock and patterned paper. Embellish with assorted stickers, photos, vellum quotes and stitching.

Jen
SMILE
loved by many
0002004
laugh
live

Chapter 3

kids

Kids are not only the subject of many scrapbook albums but they are also great scrapbookers who can contribute to the look and style of your pages. Add sentimental value and variety to your albums by having your kids add their personal touch to your pages or by creating pages of their own. This section's examples provide ideas for you to incorporate your children's artwork, letters, handwritten journaling and more into your scrapbooks.

kids

JoAnn ScrapEssentials

a flower for mom

Designer: Lily Goldsmith

Ink edges of a diecut frame and attach to patterned paper. Cover layout with patterned paper, stamps, stickers and tag. Add buckle and bookplate; finish with a flower and an inked-stencil monogram.

precious julia

Designer: Marie-Eve Bélanger

Use stamped-canvas squares to create title. Stitch fabric on cardstock to create background. Rubber stamp journaling and date. Finish with 3-D embellishments.

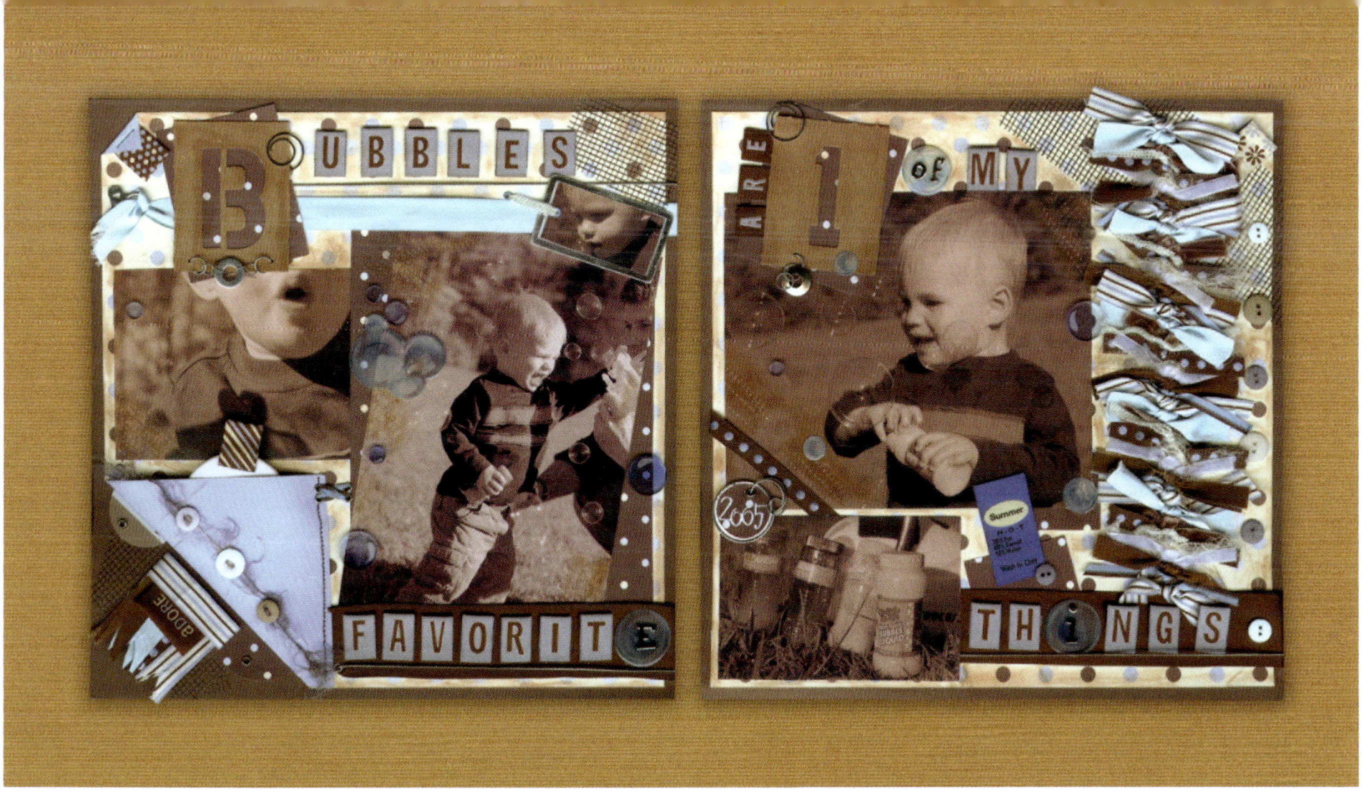

bubbles are my favorite things

Designer: Sonia Pancratz

Print photos in sepia color tones. Layer patterned paper on cardstock and ink the edges. Adhere assorted 3-D embellishments. Record your child's voice on a small recording device and place inside pocket.

Jo-Ann ScrapEssentials

bill, bugs & ed

Designer: Leah Fung

Print journaling on cardstock background. Stitch patterned paper and photo mat. Embellish with ribbons, flowers, brads, clip, photo corners and tickets.

JoAnn ScrapEssentials

strong willed

Designer: Lily Goldsmith

Layer patterned papers to create the background. Add journaling, stickers, ribbon, brads and silk flowers.

JoAnn ScrapEssentials

abby goes to gymboree

Designer: Anna Nielson

Mat photos on printed cardstock and add sticker brads. Adhere wood and metal embellishments. Top with monogram letter and leather flower.

love to swim

Designer: Rachael Giallongo

Stitch patterned paper and cardstock to create background. Print title and journaling on cardstock.

Jo-Ann ScrapEssentials

live, laugh

Designer: Kay Rogers

Layer patterned paper and transparencies to create background. Place photos into transparency frames. Embellish with tags, buttons, stickers and stapled fibers.

step 1

Layer cardstock bands and small rectangle to create background.

step 2

Mat photo on cardstock; add screw brads, sticker and ribbon knots to the mat. Create journaling with stickers and rub-ons. Embellish with ribbon band and brads. Adhere playing cards and spiral clips to layout.

step 3

Create title with labeler sticker phrases and rub-on letters. Add stickers to create date and rub-on letters for names.

Jo-Ann ScrapEssentials

my boys

Designer: NanC & Company

Create layout with textured cardstock. Mat a photo and tie ribbon knots along side. Create journaling with labeler sticker strips, rub-on letters and quote. Add playing cards and metal charms.

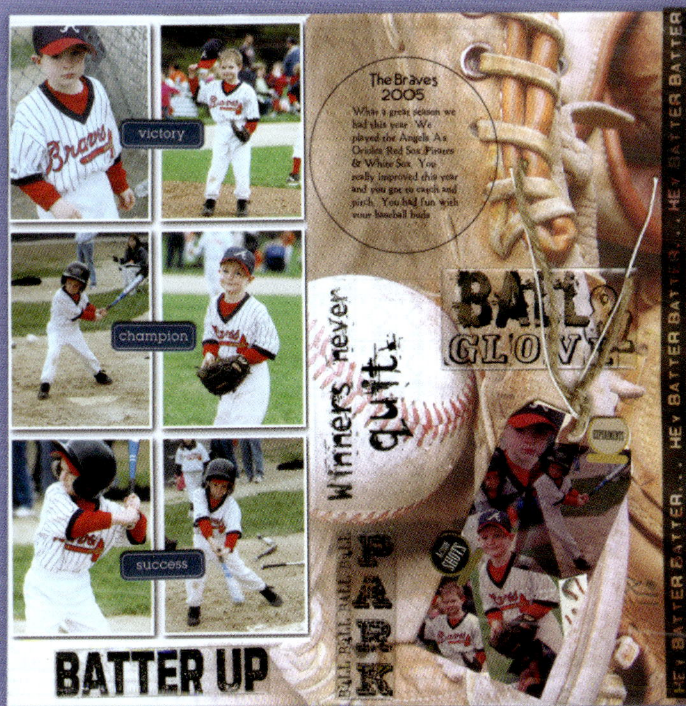

the braves 2005 season

Designer: Martha Crowther

Print trading-card sized photos and adhere to patterned paper. Create a collaged tag by layering transparencies and photos and adding fibers to the top. Embellish with metal word charms and stickers.

JoAnn ScrapEssentials

love & be loved

Designer: Leisa Tobler

Embellish background with assorted fabric bands. Print journaling on cardstock. Ink edges of photo, journaling and background. Add vellum quote, ribbon and key.

ScrapEssentials JoAnn

life

Designer: Sonia Pancratz

Cut fabric swatches and adhere to patterned paper background; sew border. Create title with painted chipboard letters. Embellish with ribbons, flowers, metal charms and buttons.

ScrapEssentials JoAnn

typical ford

Designer: Mandy Ford

Create a frame around photo with patterned paper strips. Mat journaling and embellish with brads, rub-on letters, button, sticker letters and ribbons.

boucherville

Designer: Marie-Eve Bélanger

Create title with sticker, stamp, and wooden letters. Create journaling with labeler-printed stickers and tag. Embellish with painted frame, eyelets, ribbon and epoxy clip. Make a film strip from cardstock and assorted photos.

JoAnn ScrapEssentials

loving 3

Designer: Anna Estrada Davidson

Paint chipboard shapes and coin holder. Embellish with flowers, patterned paper, button, mesh and metal letters.

JoAnn ScrapEssentials

the dance

Designer: Lisa Pace

Add sparkle to title and journaling with crystal lacquer and glitter. Create the title on a hinged journaling book. Print journaling, cut and mat on cardstock; ink the edges. Embellish with ribbons, flowers, rub-ons and metal embellishments.

imagine

Designer: Kay Rogers

Cut and layer patterned paper on cardstock. Use rub-on stitches and barcode. Mat journaling sticker; add ribbons and flower.

dancers

Designer: Janet Schroeder

Cut circle mat out of cardstock and ink edges. Adhere to layered patterned paper. Create title with patterned-paper letters. Add ribbon and large flower with acrylic circle.

what i love about having a girl

Designer: Jessica Bombaci

Layer patterned papers and stitch to cardstock. Print journaling on cardstock and attach with brads. Stamp with paint, use diecut letters for title and finish with ribbon and flower.

she wants 2 be a rock star

Designer: Karen Clark

Conceal journaling tags behind photo. Create background from patterned paper, cardstock, tags and photos. Embellish with metallic initial, bead flower and printed words.

4th grade

Designer: Sharyn Tormanen

Create journaling with metal charm words. Create title with a framed stencil, 3-D and stamped letters. Finish with ribbons and stitching.

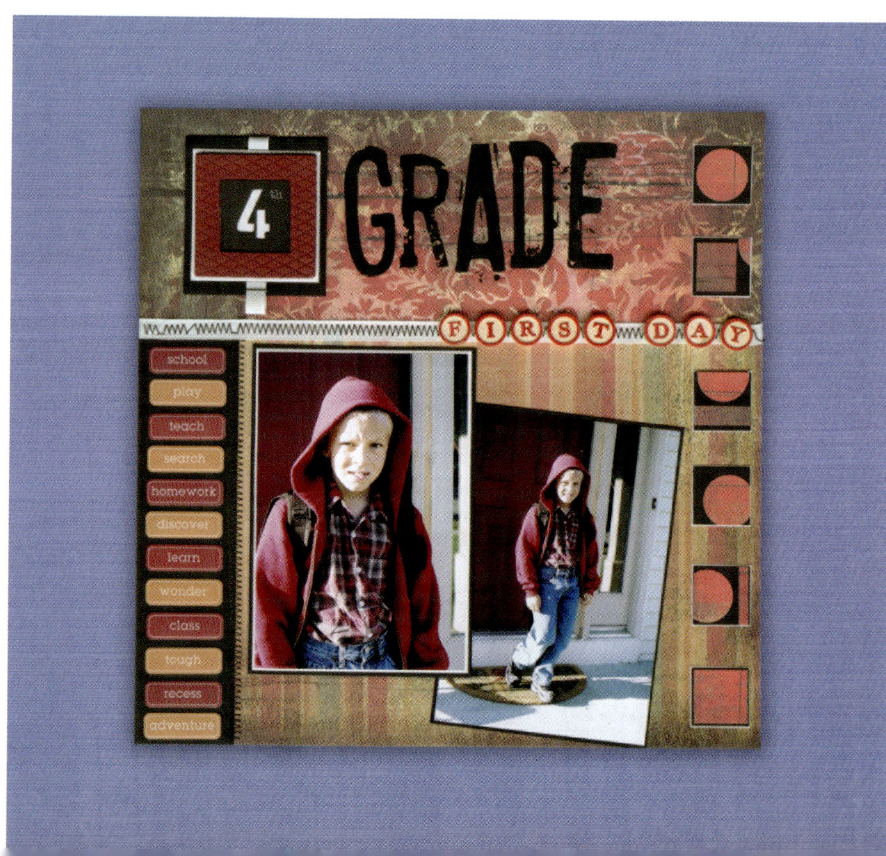

unbearable frustrations of being 3

Designer: Lynda Sturney

Create title with stamps, assorted metal letters and handwriting. Layer photos on patterned paper and mount enlarged photo to transparency. Stamp journaling and add rub-ons.

beauty in a red dress

Designer: Lily Goldsmith

Layer cardstock and patterned paper to create background. Create a title with chipboard and rub-on letters; ink and sand edges of cardstock and staple ribbons on ends. Embellish with assorted 3-D embellishments.

JoAnn ScrapEssentials

a year in the life

Designer: Leah Fung

Cut transparencies into squares, stitch to cardstock and create pockets. Print the journaling on cardstock; cut and tuck behind photos in pockets. Embellish with ribbon, flower and 3-D metal embellishments.

JoAnn ScrapEssentials

petit pianiste

Designer: Marie-Eve Bélanger

Overlap inked patterned paper to create the background. Embellish with metal bookplate, flower, ribbon, photo turns and brads. Create title with sticker letters.

delight in the journey

Designer: Becky Heisler

Cut photo and patterned paper to create a mosaic background. Create title and journaling with rub-on words and stickers. Conceal journaling under hinged photo.

heritage park

Designer: Lynda Sturney

Cut narrow strips of cardstock that extend photo lines and adhere them to patterned paper. Layer photos, sand the edges and add photo corners. Embellish with 3-D metal charms, mesh and embossed decorations.

JoAnn ScrapEssentials

art by ben

Designer: Sam Cousins

Create a child's sketch book. Cover a journal with patterned paper and a black-and-white copy of the child's artwork; mat a photo. Embellish cover with distressed stickers and a rub-on monogram. Tie closed with ribbons.

JoAnn ScrapEssentials

my family 2005

Designer: NanC & Company

Mat child's hand-drawn family portrait. Stamp names and embellish with cork stickers. Frame in glass frame.

involving kids in scrapbooking

Children are very creative and have vast imaginations. Their creativity becomes evident the first time they proudly show off their crayon drawings on the wall or perhaps after using a permanent marker on the freshly-painted front door. Because most children have artistic talent, it is important for you to give them an opportunity to showcase their creative masterpieces. Fill a box or container with crayons, markers, stickers, stamps, paper and supplies you no longer use and keep them in a convenient place for your child to use whenever he or she wants. You may also purchase special paper and sticker collections with colors and styles just for children. Let your child scrapbook special occasion mini albums or a larger personal album. Encourage your artist to draw in a sketchbook or a portfolio and to keep their special art work. Remember to record the date and journal the entries. As time passes, your child will be delighted that all their memories are preserved in their own special style.

ScrapEssentials

boy shadow box

Designer: Becky Heisler

Cover cardboard shadow box with patterned paper and fill with a photo and child's drawings. Embellish with toys and other child memorabilia.

ScrapEssentials

baby photo keepsake box

Designer: Alecia Ackerman Grimm

Adhere beads to chipboard initial. Create background with layers of frayed fabric. Tuck photo inside transparency pocket. Adhere brads to corrugated paper. Tie ribbons, add letter charm and journaling.

wonder

Designer: Maria Burke

Overlap patterned paper on cardstock. Add vellum quote, title sticker and diecut monogram. Embellish with brads and string.

making the cut

Designer: Sherry Wright

JoAnn ScrapEssentials

Adhere a special certificate and vellum envelope with lock of hair. Print journaling on cardstock and create title with rub-on letters and stamping. Finish with assorted ribbon and spiral clip.

JoAnn ScrapEssentials

love

Designer: Marie-Eve Bélanger

Cut patterned-paper blocks and adhere to cardstock. Print title on cardstock and add silk flowers with brads.

kids

JoAnn ScrapEssentials

one year

Designer: Julie Laakso

Print journaling on patterned paper and adhere to cardstock. Stitch patterned paper. Add brads, rub-on stitches, flowers and stickers.

JoAnn ScrapEssentials

love is the beauty of the soul

Designer: Pam Callaghan

Tear and sand patterned paper; adhere to stitched cardstock. Mat photo, print journaling and create title with rub-on quote. Tie ribbon across front; add metal embellishment and sticker.

this thing called love

Designer: Cheryl Baase

Create the background with layered patterned paper. Cut cardstock strip and use rub-on letters to create title. Tie ribbons and embellish with metal clip.

JoAnn ScrapEssentials

beauty

Designer: Leisa Tobler

Layer patterned papers to create the background. Print journaling on transparency paper. Create a journaling tag and conceal behind photo mat. Add ribbon knots and assorted brads.

Love is the Greatest Refreshment in Life

Chapter 4

wedding

Few life events are more anticipated than weddings. Use your scrapbooking skills to plan, organize, decorate and remember that special day. This section is filled with paper-crafting ideas from invitations to paper flower centerpieces and everything in-between designed to personalize a wedding. Cherish memories of that momentous event with an album full of wedding memorabilia and photographs. Whether you've been married for six months or forty years, it's never too late to make that one-of-a-kind wedding album.

wedding

Jo-Ann ScrapEssentials

wedding invitation

Designer: Bea Elizalde

Fold cardstock to create card and sand edges. Create a cardstock band and cover with patterned paper. Embellish with jewel-centered paper flower. Print the invitation information and adhere inside.

Jo-Ann ScrapEssentials

wedding thank you card

Designer: Bea Elizalde

Emboss and sand flower image. Create a card using complimentary patterned paper and cardstock. Finish with ribbons, rub-ons and tag.

JoAnn ScrapEssentials

wedding notebook

Designer: Bea Elizalde

Fill a spiral album with cardstock tab dividers and pockets. Embellish cover with cardstock, patterned paper, stickers and 3-D embellishments. Tie ribbon knots down spine of album. Fill the inside with wedding notes, magazine clippings and information.

JoAnn ScrapEssentials

wedding program

Designer: Bea Elizalde

Emboss a ready made card; sand image and edges. Cover spine binding with band of patterned paper. String ribbon around card and tie in a knot; attach tag. Place program information inside.

wedding

step 1

Tear mulberry paper to create flower petals and leaves. Use a diluted acrylic paint to darken edges of paper and create dimension. Curl yellow wire for flower center and attach to a long center wire.

step 2

Attach petals to wire center and wrap with floral tape. Attach leaf lower on stem and cover with floral tape.

step 3

Fill wood box with floral foam. Insert paper flowers and cover with moss. Attach ribbon and monogram charm.

Jo-Ann ScrapEssentials

floral center piece

Designer: Aven Richmond & Britney Peine

Cover a wooden box with patterned paper, ribbon and metallic accents. Top the centerpiece with handmade paper flowers.

love hanger

Designer: NanC & Company

Cover a cork square with sanded cardstock and patterned paper. Print and cut message; attach brads to the corners. Finish with rub-ons, cork letters, ribbon, staples and sanded metal key.

what i love is near at hand

Designer: NanC & Company

Cover an accordion album with patterned paper, distressed photos, ribbons, definitions and quotes. Add assorted 3-D embellishments, metals and rub-ons.

wedding

Jo-Ann ScrapEssentials

party favor suckers

Designer: Aven Richmond & Britney Peine

Cover a flower pot with adhesive ribbon and metal stickers. Fill with floral foam, moss and suckers that have messages on the leaves.

Jo-Ann ScrapEssentials

wedding favor basket

Designer: Aven Richmond & Britney Peine

Decoupage paper onto a painted wooden basket. Embellish with a homemade paper flower. Fill inside with small favors covered with patterned paper and sticker messages.

Jo-Ann ScrapEssentials

wedding keepsake box

Designer: Aven Richmond & Britney Peine

Decoupage a luggage carry-on with patterned paper, photos, metal charms and stickers.

Jo-Ann ScrapEssentials

wedding vase

Designer: Aven Richmond & Britney Peine

Cover a glass vase with torn pieces of patterned paper. Embellish with adhesive ribbon and paper flowers.

JoAnn ScrapEssentials

unconditional love

Designer: Alecia Ackerman Grimm

Create a background with patterned paper, cardstock and ribbon. Mat photo and conceal journaling tag behind. Embellish with ribbon, circle tags and metal bookplate.

JoAnn ScrapEssentials

table numbers

Designer: Julie Ann Shahin

Fold cardstock to create a square tube; add patterned paper bands. Finish with silk flowers, brads and rub-ons.

JoAnn ScrapEssentials

once in a lifetime

Designer: Alecia Ackerman Grimm

Hand cut patterned paper for title and paint around edges. Layer patterned paper and tags; stitch around the edges. Embellish with run-ons, rhinestones, brads, metal and epoxy stickers.

wedding

A wedding is a special moment in time that should always be remembered. Great care and thought must be taken when organizing and creating your wedding albums and papercrafting projects. Making your invitations, programs and thank you cards instead of buying them enhances personal, warm feelings toward those special people in your lives. In order to make your memorabilia timeless, neutral colors maybe the best choice. Color coordinate the invitation, programs, thank you cards, center pieces and party favors with the colors that you have chosen for your wedding. Make a guest registry that resembles a scrapbook album with pictures, patterned paper, cardstock and embellishments. Leave space for your guests to sign and give advice. This advice book will be something that everyone can cherish. Display the book someplace accessible so that it can be seen throughout the years. If you chose to have your wedding invitations, programs and thank you cards professionally made, you could make a wedding box to preserve all of your important treasures.

wedding

congratulations tag card

Designer: NanC & Company

JoAnn ScrapEssentials

Fold cardstock to create a large card. Cover the front with a variety of paper and embellishments. Stitch several step pockets inside; create embellished tags and tuck. Print journaling on cardstock. Embellish with ribbons, metal charms, flowers and stickers.

JoAnn ScrapEssentials

a charmed life

Designer: Linda Sobolewski

Create background with patterned paper and cardstock. Round the edge of an enlarged photo and adhere rub-ons. Create title with rub-ons, flowers and photo corners. Attach inked journaling, ribbon and metal charm.

JoAnn ScrapEssentials

celebrate

Designer: Julie Ann Shahin

Print journaling on vellum and mat to cardstock. Place photos behind printed transparency. Embellish with silk flower, 3-D metal embellishments and rhinestones.

wedding candle

Designer: Pam Callaghan

Stitch patterned paper and wrap around candle. Embellish the back of band with brads and tie a ribbon bow in the front.

JoAnn ScrapEssentials

our love will never fade

Designer: NanC & Company

Arrange squares of sanded cardstock for background. Mat photo and attach photo turns. Add title with rub-ons and matted stickers. Finish with sanded metal tags and ribbon.

bride

Designer: Heidi Knight

Compose a page on your computer. Layer the photo, paper and elements. Use the pinch command to create ribbon running through the charm. Adjust the hue and saturation.

step 1

Cut patterned-paper squares and ink the edges. Adhere to cardstock creating a mosaic background.

step 2

Mat photo on paint chip. Tie ribbon knots on side of mat and embellish with jewels. Adhere to background with adhesive foam dots; attach mini clothes pins to the top.

step 3

Mat a sticker quote onto sanded cardstock. Embellish with jewels and small patterned paper squares. Attach with foam adhesive dots.

JoAnn ScrapEssentials

together

Designer: NanC & Company

Cut and ink squares to create background. Mat photo on paint chip. Create journaling with sticker. Embellish with ribbon knots, mini clothes pins and jewels. Attach with foam adhesive dots.

wedding

wedding cards box

Designer: Jill Stenglein

Paint and ink a wooden hinged box. Create title with vellum word, stickers and stamped letters. Finish with tulle, flowers, ribbon and a 3-D sticker.

Jo-Ann ScrapEssentials

cherish bride

Designer: Becky Heisler

Create background with layered patterned paper. Add cardstock strip with sewn diamonds. Embellish with monogram rub-on, 3-D words, journaling, metal clips, photo turn and wire flower.

JoAnn ScrapEssentials

family

Designer: Mary Macaskill

Alter photo and create journaling in a computer program and print. Embellish with metal tag, brads and silk flowers.

father of the bride

Designer: Sue Fields

Enlarge photo and adhere to background. Tie ribbon over photo. Print journaling on cardstock. Create title with handkerchief folded to highlight embroidery.

BUDDY
PAL
AMIGO
friend
F
Thank You

Chapter 5

cards

Sometimes a thoughtful card is the best way to express your love, gratitude, sympathy, excitement, apology or congratulations. Homemade cards are thoughtful gifts and can make the moment when store-bought cards just won't do. This section features a variety of styles, sizes and shapes of cards for all occasions. Find step-by-step instructions on how to make and embellish cards or just add to your portfolio of card-making ideas.

JoAnn ScrapEssentials

friendship card

Designer: Becky Heisler

Cut two pieces of cardstock, punch holes on top and tie ribbons to connect. Create background with patterned paper and cardstock triangles. Attach frame, quote and stickers. Finish with heart clip and flower.

JoAnn ScrapEssentials

fabric card

Designer: Sherry Wright

Stitch fabric squares on front of card. Punch holes along the top edge, thread and tie fabric strips and fiber.

p&k always

Designer: Pam Callaghan

Create a pocket card with sewn cardstock. Round the corners of paper squares and adhere to the pocket. Create a pull out card and staple oval to top. Finish with stapled ribbons, flower, 3-D letters and rub-ons.

u r one in a million

Designer: NanC & Company

Create a sliding card by attaching layered ribbon to the cardstock so that a card can slide in and out of the ribbon. Create the slide-in with inked and torn patterned paper and cardstock. Create title with rub-ons, stickers, and page pebble. Finish with a handwritten message.

JoAnn ScrapEssentials

baby boy tin

Designer: NanC & Company

Paint and sand a metal tin. Cover outside with patterned paper and rub-ons. Finish with 3-D embellishments and buttons. Decorate the inside with patterned paper. Write a message on sanded cardstock and attach with an adhesive foam dot. Tie closed with ribbon.

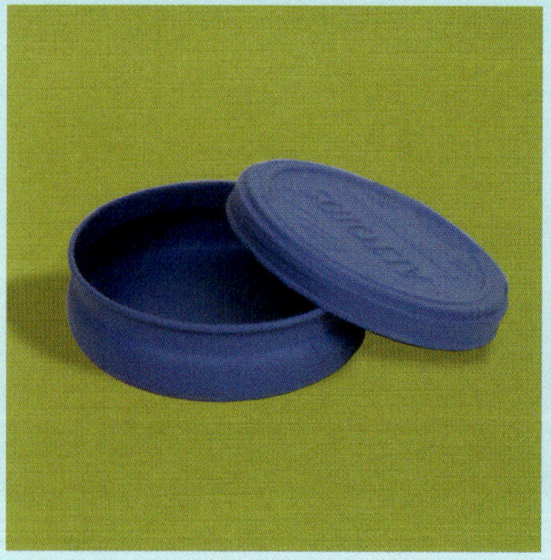

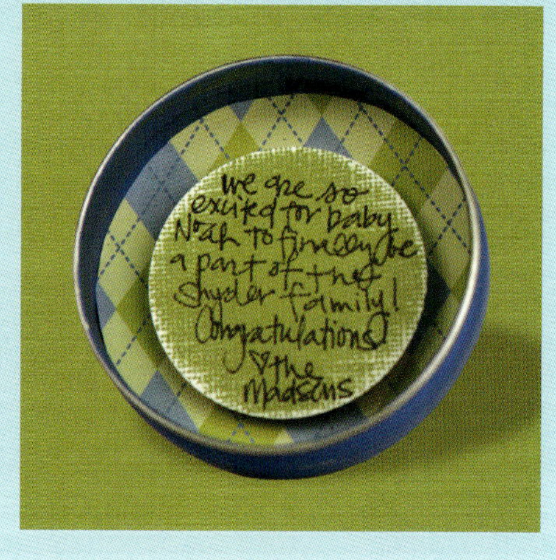

step 1

Paint the inside and outside of a mint tin.

step 2

Decorate cover with patterned paper, rub-ons, acrylic accents and metal word.

step 3

Fill inside can with patterned paper and sanded cardstock message. Adhere with an adhesive foam dot.

summer card

Designer: Linda Beeson

Cut and adhere cardstock blocks to card. Apply rub-on words; add stickers and paper flowers.

birthday wish

Designer: Irene Nelson

Fold patterned paper to create a pocket inside. Sand and ink the edges. Decorate the front with a button-topped flower and hanging epoxy tag. Embellish the inside with brads and a rub-on phrase; tuck a decorative tag in the pocket.

hey love card

Designer: NanC & Company

Sand the edges of a textured cardstock card and four blocks. Stitch around each shape. Add metal embellishment, knotted buttons, tied ribbon and rub-on words.

Jo-Ann ScrapEssentials

love you tag

Designer: Sandra Helder

Create a tag with scraps of patterned paper; round the corners and ink. Sand and ink letter stickers. Cover fibers with flower and brad.

Jo-Ann ScrapEssentials

baby card

Designer: Malena Ogden

Adhere patterned paper and cardstock to card. Embellish with staples and buttons. Fill metal bookplate with sticker letters and attach with brads.

Jo-Ann ScrapEssentials

friends card

Designer: Lisa Pace

Create a card with cardstock figures. Embellish with patterned paper, brads, fiber, beads and rickrack.

the magic of christmas

Designer: Linda Beeson

Fold cardstock to create card and adhere patterned paper. Place snowman sticker on circle and add metal brad. Create title with rub-on words.

JoAnn ScrapEssentials

fabric pocket & tag

Designer: Sam Cousins

Cover a library pocket and tag with fabric. Decorate tag with stapled fabric strips, stickers, ribbon and snowflakes. Tuck the tag inside a sticker embellished pocket.

let it snow

Designer: Kate Thaete

Fold cardstock in half to create a card. Adhere a snowman head and a nose made from cardstock; add dimension to the nose with chalk lines. Use buttons to create eyes. Print a message repeatedly with a labeler and attach to fit card.

JoAnn ScrapEssentials

snowflake card

Designer: Susan Stringfellow

Tie ribbon onto painted wood snowflake; adhere metal snowflake on top. Create background with patterned paper and metal strip.

JoAnn ScrapEssentials

christmas card

Designer: Irene Nelson

Overlap patterned paper to create background. Fill circle with hanging metal charm. Adhere rectangle page pebble over corner of matted patterned paper.

JoAnn ScrapEssentials

may your holidays be filled

Designer: NanC & Company

Sand the edges of a cardstock card. Fill circles with patterned paper, envelope seals and clear page pebbles. Frame quote stickers with paper bookplate and add brads. Hand stitch border.

smile card

Designer: Irene Nelson

Cover cardstock card with patterned paper. Adhere ribbon and staple edges. Loop ribbon through charm and adhere.

christmas tag & sleeve

Designer: NanC & Company

Jo-Ann ScrapEssentials

Create a pocket out of patterned paper. Embellish with metal tag, letter and rickrack. Make a tag to fit inside with cardstock, patterned paper, stickers and rub-ons. Top with fiber and ribbon.

you inspire me

Designer: Sarah Adams

Fold cardstock in half to create card and cover with patterned paper strips. Adhere woven and paper tag, ribbon, flower, brads and stickers.

JoAnn ScrapEssentials

star envelope card

Designer: NanC & Company

Cut a cardstock envelope and emboss star pattern on the closed flaps. Cut and sand the star and attach to cover. Sand and ink framed photo inside. Embellish with metal tag and diecut letters.

happy birthday coaster card

Designer: Maria Burke

Cover coasters with patterned paper. Embellish with printed and handwritten journaling, ribbon and brads. Punch a hole in the corners and tie together with ribbon.

Jo-Ann ScrapEssentials

card organizer

Designer: NanC & Company

Adorn a divided holder to organize handmade cards. Embellish cover with patterned paper, cardstock, assorted letters and metal embellishments. Decorate inside with printed quote and tabs.

JoAnn ScrapEssentials

monogram card

Designer: Irene Nelson

Sand and ink different shapes of patterned paper and arrange on to card. Mat monogram rub-on and staple ribbons on top edge.

JoAnn ScrapEssentials

get well soon

Designer: NanC & Company

Cover a pre-made gatefold card with ripped-patterned paper; ink and sand the edges. Embellish with ribbons, knotted-buttons and brads. Personalized a message with stickers. Finish center circle with brads, ribbon and a clear epoxy circle.

Jo-Ann ScrapEssentials

get well

Designer: Irene Nelson

Adhere patterned paper to card; sand and ink the edges. Punch holes in patterned paper and tie ribbon knots through. Embellish card with inked cardstock, metal tag and epoxy circle.

Jo-Ann ScrapEssentials

happy thanksgiving 2day

Designer: NanC & Company

Fold cardstock in half to create a card. Embellish with assorted letter stickers, rub-ons, cork and 3-D metals. Ink and sand various patterned papers and cardstock. Hand stitch design on ribbons and add brads. Embellish inside card.

JoAnn ScrapEssentials

monogram birthday card

Designer: NanC & Company

Create an accordion monogram card. Layer assorted patterned paper and cardstock; sand and ink the edges. Embellish with cork letters, stickers, rub-ons, ribbon knots, brads and handwriting. Attach accordion card together with ribbon and hold it closed with an oval spiral clip.

step 1

Cut the outline of six cardstock letters to make an accordion card. Cut the inside curves of half of the letters. Place three letters aside.

step 2

On three of the letters, adhere patterned paper and cardstock to the front. Heavily ink and sand the surfaces.

step 3

Embellish the card with cork letters, stickers, rub-ons, ribbon knots, brads and handwriting. Attach thick ribbon to the back of the embellished card. Take the remaining cardstock letters and place behind the embellished letters so that the ribbon is covered.

Jo-Ann ScrapEssentials

relax card

Designer: Toni Boucha

Cover patterned cardstock with mesh. Mat photo stickers and adhere to card; add brads and apply a rub-on word for title

Jo-Ann ScrapEssentials

happy birthday papa

Designer: NanC & Company

Layer assorted ribbon on an inked card. Use rub-ons and stickers for a personalized message. Embellish metal tag with cork stickers and patterned paper; attach tag with ribbon bands and brads.

i love you valentine's tag

Designer: Elizabeth Lee

Cut circle from cardstock and stamp background. Cover with paper strips, ribbon, lace and flower. Top with chipboard letter and photo turn.

JoAnn ScrapEssentials

friend thank you card

Designer: NanC & Company

Create the background by stitching patterned paper to cardstock. Embellish with assorted sticker words, rub-on letters and labeler words. Inside the card create a stitched pocket; embellish front with epoxy stickers. Tuck decorated tag inside.

Jo-Ann ScrapEssentials

bonjour card

Designer: Susan Stringfellow

Enhance a pre-made scalloped card; ink puzzle pieces, apply embossing powder and heat. Stamp title and use rub-on decals. Tie ribbon and add metal charm.

Jo-Ann ScrapEssentials

liz

Designer: NanC & Company

Fold orange cardstock in half to create card. Layer torn patterned paper and cardstock. Sand the paper, metal letters and brads. Finish with matted metal letters, ribbon knots and brads.

Jo-Ann ScrapEssentials

hi card

Designer: NanC & Company

Sand, ink, and zigzag stitch cardstock. Embellish with layered ribbon and puzzle piece.

all boy card

Designer: NanC & Company

Cut patterned paper pocket and stitch to cardstock. Create title with sticker. Rip patterned paper and adhere down spine; punch holes and tie through ribbon. Embellish cardstock tag with ribbon knot and metal charm; tuck inside pocket.

you hold the key to my heart card

Designer: NanC & Company

Add cardstock band to a pre-made card and sand edges. Add ribbon knots and metal key. Create title with 3-D stickers, stamped cardstock and rub-on letters.

it's your day card

Designer: Cindy Smith

Cover cardstock with patterned paper and stickers. Fill metal tag with matted cardstock stickers, eyelets and a brad.

Chapter 6

home décor

Spread charm throughout your home with scrapbooking-inspired home décor. There are countless ways to use your scrapbooking products and techniques to complete projects around your home. Build upon these ideas with your own unique ideas for decorating your home. Altering frames, decoupaging chairs and creating magnetic boards are just a few of the ideas featured on the following pages.

be frame

Designer: Cindy Smith

Cover canvas frame with patterned paper strips, inked photos and buttons. Tie ribbon to connect frames. Paint and sand letters and adhere to front.

Jo-Ann ScrapEssentials

thank heaven for little girls

Designer: Tistann Graves

Stain edges of canvas, wood tag and flower with tea stain. Decoupage patterned paper and photo on background.

Jo-Ann ScrapEssentials

ava wood board

Designer: Anna Nielson

Cover a wood board with patterned paper and rub-on words. Personalize with assorted 3-D embellishments.

Jo-Ann ScrapEssentials

photo cubes

Designer: Leah Fung

Cover sides of wooden blocks with assorted patterned paper. Adhere metal embellishments on top of photo and tie ribbon in a knot.

home décor

altered summer frames

Designer: Netalia LaConti-Riggle

Decoupage wooden frames with sanded textured cardstock. Create title and journaling with rub-on words.

mosiac clock

Designer: Julie Ann Shahin

Decoupage cardstock squares in a star design to a clock. Reattach clock hands to the clock movement.

Jo-Ann ScrapEssentials

panama city tin hanger

Designer: Alecia Ackerman Grimm

Fill tin compartments with an assortment of embellishments; apply stickers and charms to the outside. Attach a photo, word stickers and seashells; finish with a twill-ribbon hanger.

Jo-Ann ScrapEssentials

grow shadow box

Designer: Sam Cousins

Paint outside of wood shadow box, sand and add ribbon. Fill inside with sanded cardstock, rub-on letters and assorted 3-D flower embellishments.

home décor

JoAnn ScrapEssentials

key holder

Designer: Cindy Smith

Decoupage floral paper to key holder. Attach ribbon, flowers, buttons and metal letters.

chair

Designer: Aven Richmond & Britney Peine

Decoupage an assortment of torn patterned papers to the surface of a wood chair.

calendar

Designer: NanC & Company

Paint wooden calendar. Layer patterned paper, photo and rub-on letters for background. Adhere a monogram fabric pocket to the top of the calendar to hold extra calendar pieces. Create number and picture graphics with rub-ons and 3-D embellishments.

glam girl wall décor

Designer: Julie Ann Shahin

Embellish a photo holder. Add ribbon, flowers, brads and buttons. Fill in glasses with patterned paper.

disney frame

Designer: Susan Stringfellow

Cover a wood frame with patterned paper; ink the edges. Tie ribbon bow on side; attach sequins, metal tag and clip. Ink the edges of the 3-D stickers and attach to the frame.

night light

Designer: Cindy Smith

Cover a night light shade with patterned paper, ribbon, rickrack and knotted buttons.

JoAnn ScrapEssentials

baby boy light switch

Designer: Cindy Smith

Sand and paint wood light switch. Adhere patterned paper with decoupage. Sand edges lightly, attach ribbon, a metal letter and sticker with foam tape.

JoAnn ScrapEssentials

clock

Designer: Cindy Smith

Embellish, paint and adhere patterned paper to a wooden clock. Remove center from silk flower and place through clock movements. Tie ribbon bow and add letter brad.

JoAnn ScrapEssentials

patchwork magnet board

Designer: NanC & Company

Paint the wood frame of a magnet board. Fill inside with squares of inked patterned paper to create a patchwork look. Create magnents with 3-D metal embellishments and rub-on monogram.

JoAnn ScrapEssentials

towel holder

Designer: Anna Estrada Davidson

Decoupage wood hook with patterned paper and quote. Add ribbon tie and rhinestone jewel.

JoAnn ScrapEssentials

family vacation fund

Designer: NanC & Company

Stitch ribbon to patterned paper creating small pleats. Create title with rub-ons, metals, stamps and acrylic letters. Decorate the lid with stapled ribbons and patterned paper.

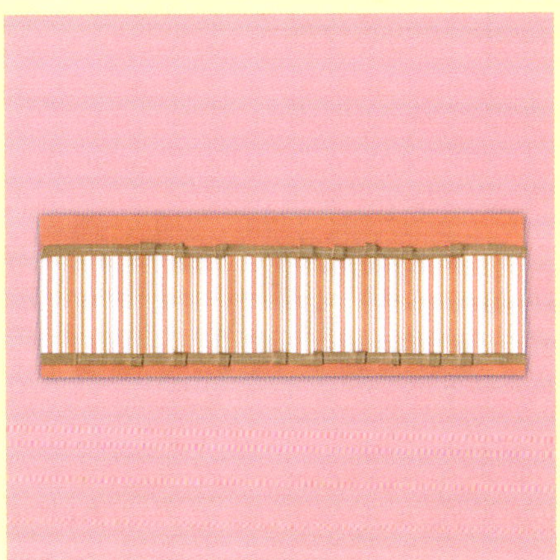

step 1

Cut layered patterned paper slightly larger than the circumference of a paint tin; ink and sand the edges. While making small tucks, stitch ribbon onto paper.

step 2

Adhere the embellished patterned paper to paint can. Cover the lid with patterned paper and attach stapled ribbon ties.

step 3

Embellish with acrylic words, stamps, metal charms and rub-on letters.

home décor

tissue box

Designer: Julie Ann Shahin

Decoupage patterned paper to a cardstock tissue box cover. Adhere a silk flower to the front.

breakfast tray

Designer: NanC & Company

JoAnn ScrapEssentials

Paint a breakfast tray, sand the edges and tie ribbon knots on handle. Print photo on textured cardstock. Decoupage photo, patterned paper, rub-on letters and quotes.

Home Décor

Home interiors can be influenced by your scrapbooking style. Scrapbook papers and embellishments have become so beautiful and sophisticated that you shouldn't just use them in your scrapbooks. Embellish items around your home or think of new uses for items that you see everyday. Create magnets out of charms, cover frames with patterned paper or alter a piece of furniture. Expand your decorating and let it be a reflection of you.

decoupage tip

Decoupage is an exciting way to add variety to your papercrafting. Decoupage is a milk like substance used for adhering photos, patterned paper, fabric or embellishments to different kinds of mediums. Start with a thin layer of adhesive on the object that you decorating; then add another layer directly onto photos, paper, fabric, etc. Finish with one or more layers for a protective coat. For best results, use several layers of decoupage.

waste basket

Designer: Julie Ann Shahin

Attach a band of patterned paper to a cardstock garbage can. Add layers of decoupage to the entire garbage can for a protective covering. Decorate with a silk flower.

jewelry box

Designer: NanC & Company

Create a jewelry box with floral patterned paper. Attach jewels to accent parts of the flower. Cut cardstock into flowers that imitate the floral paper and adhere to the top of the jewelry box.

baby picture frames

Designer: NanC & Company

Cover frames with patterned paper. Create title with rub-on and acrylic words; embellish with buttons and metal accents.

Jo-Ann ScrapEssentials

riley's boat

Designer: Diana Lyn McGraw

Fill a wooden boat with matted photos, flowers, fiber, sea shells and fabric. Finish with ribbon and metal letters.

wood letters

Designer: Lana Bisson

Jo-Ann ScrapEssentials

Cover wooden letters with patterned paper. Add assorted 3-D embellishments, ribbons, handwriting and rub-ons.

McKay
FaMiLy
MCKAY

Chapter 7

heritage

Preserve your cherished family heritage with thoughtfully-constructed scrapbooks. There is no better way to connect generations than by preserving your life stories and traditions with those of your progenitors for future generations. Create your own heritage albums and leave for your children a legacy of remembering and treasuring. Learn how to preserve your heritage artistically in this section that covers heritage albums, shadow boxes and picture frames.

Jo-Ann ScrapEssentials

christmas box

Designer: NanC & Company

Cover hatbox top with photos, treasure tape and diamond beads. Paint wooden letters; sand and tie ribbon bows. Embellish sides with torn paper, buttons, flower and tag.

Jo-Ann ScrapEssentials

heritage journal

Designer: NanC & Company

Cover album with patterned paper and a torn cardstock spine; ink and sand the edges. Add adhesive photo corners to manipulated photo. Embellish with ribbons, 3-D stickers, tags, brads, metal charms and painted design.

Jo-Ann ScrapEssentials

williams sisters

Designer: NanC & Company

Mat vintage photo on patterned paper and adhere to cardstock; ink and sand the edges. Add 3-D metal embellishments, decorative tag, rub-ons and stickers for journaling.

Jo-Ann ScrapEssentials

memories of grandma

Designer: Becky Heisler

Print a photo in sepia tones and print journaling on textured cardstock. Border journaling and background with ribbon. Add flower, metal charms and ribbon knot.

JoAnn ScrapEssentials

what are little girls made of?

Designer: Pam Callaghan

Use a computer photo program to enhance a vintage photo. Trim frame around photo, cut corners, sew together and tie ribbon. Stitch and ink background papers. Print journaling on transparency, add vellum envelope, ribbon and brad.

JoAnn ScrapEssentials

family time heritage notebook

Designer: Melissa Tubb

Alter spiral journal with inked cardstock and patterned paper. Add stamped tag, stickers, 3-D embellishments and fibers.

JoAnn ScrapEssentials

grandma & grandpa

Designer: Sue Rhinehart

Layer pattern paper and inked vintage ephemera on cardstock to create background. Add photos and journaling. Use gold embossing enamel to create a 3-D-metal effect on embellishments.

JoAnn ScrapEssentials

sisters

Designer: Pam Callaghan

Layer patterned paper, cut into circle and mat with cardstock. Sand and ink the cardstock edges. Stitch around circle and photo mats. Embellish with ribbon, 3-D letters and sticker.

heritage

vintage mini album

Designer: Ghislaine Vincent

JoAnn ScrapEssentials

Alter a mini album with curled patterned paper "aged" with ink. Embellish cover with ribbon, flower and charm. Cover inside pages with patterned paper, ribbons, metal embellishments, button, fabric and flowers. Tie closed with ribbons.

preserving memories

Creating heritage albums is a way of linking the past to the present. If you are fortunate enough to have boxes of photos and mementos from your family, grandparents or ancestors, you can create a variety of family heirlooms that will last forever. Even though old photos typically have problems with clarity and quality, you can scan any limited or poor condition photos and save them on your computer. Colors may be digitally enhanced and tears or missing pieces can be repaired. Consider yourself a family historian and look beyond the photos to tell your ancestors' stories. Include interesting things about their lives, hobbies, talents, education and occupations. Emphasize personal traits and unique personalities. Trace the origins of family traditions. Personal letters, mementos or the backs of photos often contain a wealth of information. A heritage album will touch the hearts of each person who reads it, giving them a sense of belonging and an appreciation of their unique and wonderful heritage.

heritage

heritage shadow box

Designer: Anna Estrada Davidson

Cover a shadow box frame with patterned paper. Adhere patterned paper, vellum quote, pin and jewel inside. Place rub-on quote directly on glass.

thanksgiving card

Designer: NanC & Company

Fold cardstock in half to create a card. Cover front with patterned paper. Zigzag stitch a band of cardstock and text paper. Double mat a vintage image, add brads to the corners. Sand the edges of card and image.

Jo-Ann ScrapEssentials

pieces of the past

Designer: Susan Stringfellow

Print journaling on transparency and paint the back side. Cover chipboard puzzle pieces with paper. Layer puzzle pieces, fabric squares, lace and metal charm. Stamp on ribbons and attach to photos.

Jo-Ann ScrapEssentials

school days

Designer: Susan Stringfellow

Layer paper, photos, journaling, lace, ribbon, flowers and chipboard letters to make a collage. Stitch around patterned paper and vintage image. Create title with painted metal letters.

heritage

inspire

Designer: Leisure Arts

Create a pocket card from a playing card and patterned paper. Embellish with a quote, metal accent and flower. Tuck two embellished tags covered with heritage patterns and topped with stapled ribbons.

far away

Designer: Leisure Arts

Create a matchbook out of playing cards. Cover with patterned paper and title printed on cardstock.

pocket full of memories

Designer: Leisure Arts

Cover a playing card with patterned paper and stamped image. Create stacked pockets to hold small photos. Finish with stickers.

Jo-Ann ScrapEssentials

franklin heritage frame

Designer: Cindy Smith

Alter a wood frame with torn patterned paper and age with walnut ink. Attach twill ribbon with metal push pin and metal ribbon slides.

Jo-Ann ScrapEssentials

roots

Designer: Jessi Lane

Cut cardstock squares and adhere to background. Stamp and use rub-on letters for journaling. Embellish with buttons, decorative clip, flowers, acrylic circle and stapled rickrack.

Jo-Ann ScrapEssentials

fathers

Designer: Alecia Ackerman Grimm

Layer patterned paper and photos for background. Create title and captions with rub-on and cork letters. Handwrite journaling.

Jo-Ann ScrapEssentials

vintage card

Designer: NanC & Company

Stitch a ready-made window card to create a pocket envelope. Embellish with patterned paper, ribbon and tag. Cut a tag and top with ribbons. Finish with a vintage image sticker, patterned paper and metal clips.

Jo-Ann ScrapEssentials

love canvas

Designer: Lily Goldsmith

Alter a canvas with patterned and tissue papers. Add assorted 3-D embellishments and metals between layers of wax applied with a stiff brush.

2005 has come and gone,
it went by far too fast.
So please come and join us
to kick off 2006 with a blast!
We will have dinner and drinks,
dancing and laughter too.
We hope you can make it,
It wouldn't be the same without you!
7 p.m. on December 31st, 2005
The Diak Residence
19690 Belmont Way
Please R.S.V.P: 720-555-0304
HAPPY NEW YEAR
D
Jeffrey Holder
Denise Holder

Chapter 8

party & holiday

Who doesn't love a party? Celebrate your good times in style with thoughtful additions to your festivities. Coordinate party plans with matching place cards, invitations, menus and party favors. Take note of the following varied ideas for creating invitations, party favors and for scrapbooking photographs after the party. This section is full of fun ideas to make your parties and holiday celebrations a hit and have everybody anxiously awaiting your next bash.

girls' night out invitation

Designer: Julie Ann Shahin

Fold printed vellum to create envelope sleeve. Adhere a cardstock band and sticker. Print journaling on card and embellish with stickers.

JoAnn ScrapEssentials

"irish luck" blocks

Designer: NanC & Company

Paint blocks and sand edges. Create journaling with rub-on letters.

eggs to dye for

Designer: Sandi Minchuk

Dry brush paint and ink on cardstock background. Mat photo with inked and torn paper. Add cardstock-sticker tags, fibers and brads. Print, cut and sew journaling strips on page.

easter tin basket

Designer: NanC & Company

Cover paint can with sewn and distressed patterned paper. Tie fiber knots on handle. Attach vintage image on tag; embellish with safety pins, ribbon, photo corners and micro beads.

Jo-Ann ScrapEssentials

beach party invitation

Designer: Dana DiGennaro

Fold cardstock in half to create card. Embellish with stickers, flower and epoxy circle.

Jo-Ann ScrapEssentials

slumber party invitation

Designer: Leah Fung

Create a party invitation door hanger. Stitch patterned paper for background; outline circle opening with brad-centered flowers. Print journaling on cardstock and attach with brads, ribbon and key chain.

aloha invitation

Designer: Sam Cousins

Embellish a ready-made scalloped card. Adhere "aloha" fabric patch and silk flower to cardstock. Punch holes in scallops, tie raffia and add metal charm. Add stickers and photo corners.

flip into summer

Designer: Carolyn Lontin

Tie assorted ribbon knots on straps of flip flop. Adhere flower and paper charms. Handwrite journaling on tags topped with brads.

make a wish

Designer: Kristen Swain

Cut out chipboard letters and numbers, paint and add polka dots. Create background with patterned paper and cardstock. Embellish with metal words, ribbon, button and printed journaling.

Jo-Ann ScrapEssentials

party favor purse

Designer: Tiffany Willyerd

Fold paper purse and add ribbon for handles. Embellish with ribbon fringe and 3-D charms.

step 1

Cut patterned paper to fit inside the DVD case. Heavily ink and sand the edges.

step 2

Decorate the cover with inked-textured cardstock, sanded-metal letters, stickers and rub-ons. Tie with ribbon, add fabric label and brads.

step 3

Create a menu for the DVD. Handwrite, stamp and add stickers for journaling. Embellish with matted rub-on monogram and brads. Cover disc with sanded cardstock and handwriting.

JoAnn ScrapEssentials

birthday bash dvd case

Designer: NanC & Company

Alter a DVD case with patterned paper and cardstock; ink and sand the edges. Personalize the cover, menu and DVD with stamps, ribbons, stickers and metal. Slip into the protective cover.

ScrapEssentials

barbecue tin

Designer: Carolyn Lontin

Cover tin with patterned paper and tied ribbons. Adhere 3-D embellishments and rub-on letters.

ScrapEssentials

barbecue menu

Designer: Carolyn Lontin

Fill frame with photo and menu printed on patterned paper. Embellish with 3-D stickers.

proud to be an american

Designer: Mikki Livanos

Create background with digital paper. Cut out star shape and place inside larger star. Add depth with drop shadow and texture.

july fourth celebration

Designer: Susan Hubbs

Alter photo on computer photo program to create a leather effect; print and mat. Create background with patterned paper and photos. Embellish with ribbon bands, brads and 3-D metal embellishments.

anniversary party invitation

Designer: Pam Callaghan

Fold and ink cardstock to create card. Cover patterned paper with circle cardstock. Mat photo on cardstock and loop ribbon through eyelets. Embellish envelope with patterned paper and ribbon.

halloween decoration

Designer: NanC & Company

Cover wood initial with patterned paper and sand edges. Ink cork letters. Embellish with ribbons, buttons, paper clips, safety pin and rub-on words.

JoAnn ScrapEssentials

he-he halloween invitation

Designer: Irene Nelson

Cover chipboards with patterned paper; bind together with tulle-strip hinges. Embellish the inside with pocket and tag, ribbon, stamped words and 3-D charm. Sand and mat an embossed image on layered cardstock and patterned paper.

fairy

Designer: Kristen Swain

Layer and ink patterned paper for background. Create title with sticker letters. Print journaling on cardstock and arrange photos on top. Embellish with ribbons and embossed metals.

party & holiday

JoAnn ScrapEssentials

halloween card & envelope

Designer: Susan Stringfellow

Create invitation with stamped image. Adhere to inked patterned paper and cardstock. Embellish with ribbon attached with brads. Attach inked stamped tag. Make envelope with inked cardstock and patterned paper.

JoAnn ScrapEssentials

halloween box

Designer: Susan Stringfellow

Stamp image on cardstock; ink, mat and adhere to patterned paper. Embellish with brads. Create tag and attach with jump ring and ribbon.

Jo-Ann ScrapEssentials

autumn

Designer: Jenny Adams Powers

Mat a photo on cardstock, journal on tags and apply metal epoxy stickers. Create title with stencil monogram; rub-on words and buttons.

remember fall

Designer: Kay Rogers

Create background with layers of patterned paper and mesh. Print photo of trees onto patterned cardstock and use as a background mat. Embellish with fibers, brads, 3-D letters and metal leaf.

thanksgiving place card

Designer: Leisa Tobler

Print name on cardstock. Embellish with gold-embossed stamp, twig and silk flower.

Jo-Ann ScrapEssentials

menu

Designer: Leisa Tobler

Print journaling on cardstock and ink edges. Create background with gold-embossed cardstock. Embellish with silk flowers, brads and raffia fiber knots.

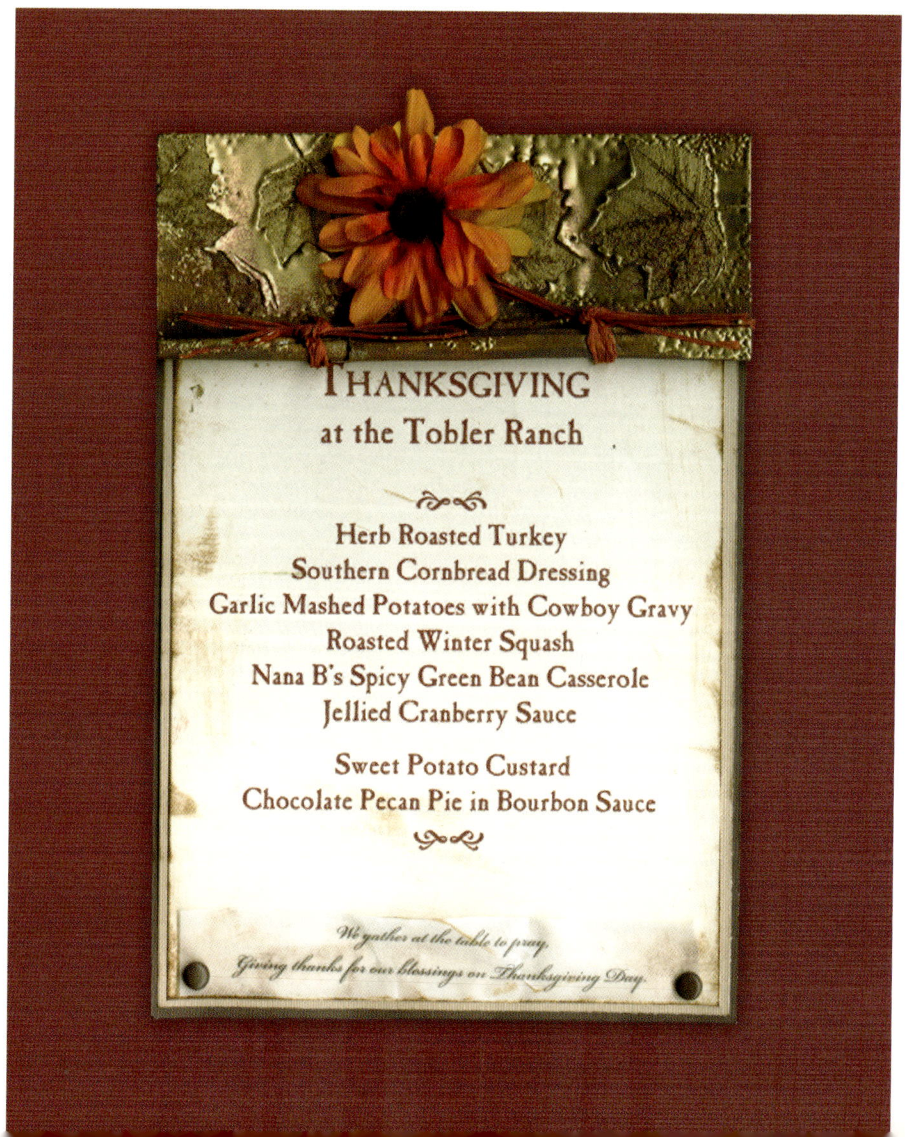

thanksgiving tag

Designer: Leisa Tobler

Create tag with cardstock. Stamp leaf on to heated gold-embossing powder. Add vellum quote, silk flower, raffia and brad.

party invitation

Designer: Leisa Tobler

Stamp on heated embossing powder to create leaf image. Embellish with silk flower, brads, twig and raffia knots.

christmas eve

Designer: Kristen Swain

Emboss metal background; layer with patterned paper. Print journaling on vellum. Embellish with matted photos, 3-D embellishments and stapled ribbon.

christmas invitation

Designer: Julie McGuffie, Scrapbook Memories Host

Diecut sunburst shape. Wrap gold thread around each sunburst and add button. Adhere to crimped paper; mat with textured cardstock.

camp christmas morning

Designer: Maria Gallardo-Williams

Adhere patterned paper and cardstock to create background. Ink edges of photo and photo mats. Use word stickers to create border and add epoxy stickers.

JoAnn ScrapEssentials

things to do before christmas chalkboard

Designer: NanC & Company

Embellish chalk board with patterned paper and ribbon. Adhere journaling stickers on ribbon. Paint metal embellishment and add monogram sticker. Embellish with stapled ribbon and matted number.

JoAnn ScrapEssentials

christmas gift bag

Designer: Alecia Ackerman Grimm

Cover gift bag with patterned paper. Embellish with buttons, flowers and rhinestones. Create title with stickers and rub-on letters; frame with ribbon. Tie ribbon and tag to the handle.

christmas tree

Designer: Alecia Ackerman Grimm

JoAnn ScrapEssentials

Cover wire tree with scrapbook embellishments. Cover tags with stickers, vellum quote and cork letters. Adhere mini flowers.

Jo-Ann ScrapEssentials

christmas magnet

Designer: Alecia Ackerman Grimm

Cut patterned paper in a stocking shape and adhere to magnet sheet; ink the edges. Add ribbon, flower, jewel and tag embellishment.

Jo-Ann ScrapEssentials

christmas stocking invitation

Designer: Alecia Ackerman Grimm

Embellish stocking diecut with tied ribbon, tags, flower and safety pin. Adhere to patterned paper background to form a pocket. Tuck in decorative tag; create title with stickers.

Jo-Ann ScrapEssentials

resolutions 2005

Designer: Alecia Ackerman Grimm

Adhere patterned paper to cardstock background. Embellish journaling strips and blocks with assorted 3-D embellishments. Fill chipboard coin holder with photos, stickers and tags. Stamp and handwrite journaling.

new year's place cards

Designer: EK Success

Layer cardstock and adhere printed vellum. Embellish with a 3-D sticker.

new year's party favor

Designer: EK Success

Cut cardstock to create a rectangle container. Embellish the front with layered cardstock and a 3-D embellishment. Fill box with streamers and party favors.

new year's party invitation

Designer: EK Success

Adhere printed vellum on matted cardstock background. Add ribbon and a 3-D sticker embellishments.

with a
KISS
let us set out for an unknown world
BEACH
And
a Dance
Good Morning to My Husband!

Chapter 9

photo manipulation

Scrapbookers constantly manipulate photographs. We tear edges, tint black and white pictures with color and print photographs onto transparencies. Software programs, digital cameras and scanners have made manipulating digital photos increasingly easy and rewarding. Find great ideas for digitally editing photos to fit the mood of your scrapbook pages in this section. Learn how to create entire scrapbook pages digitally.

photo manipulation

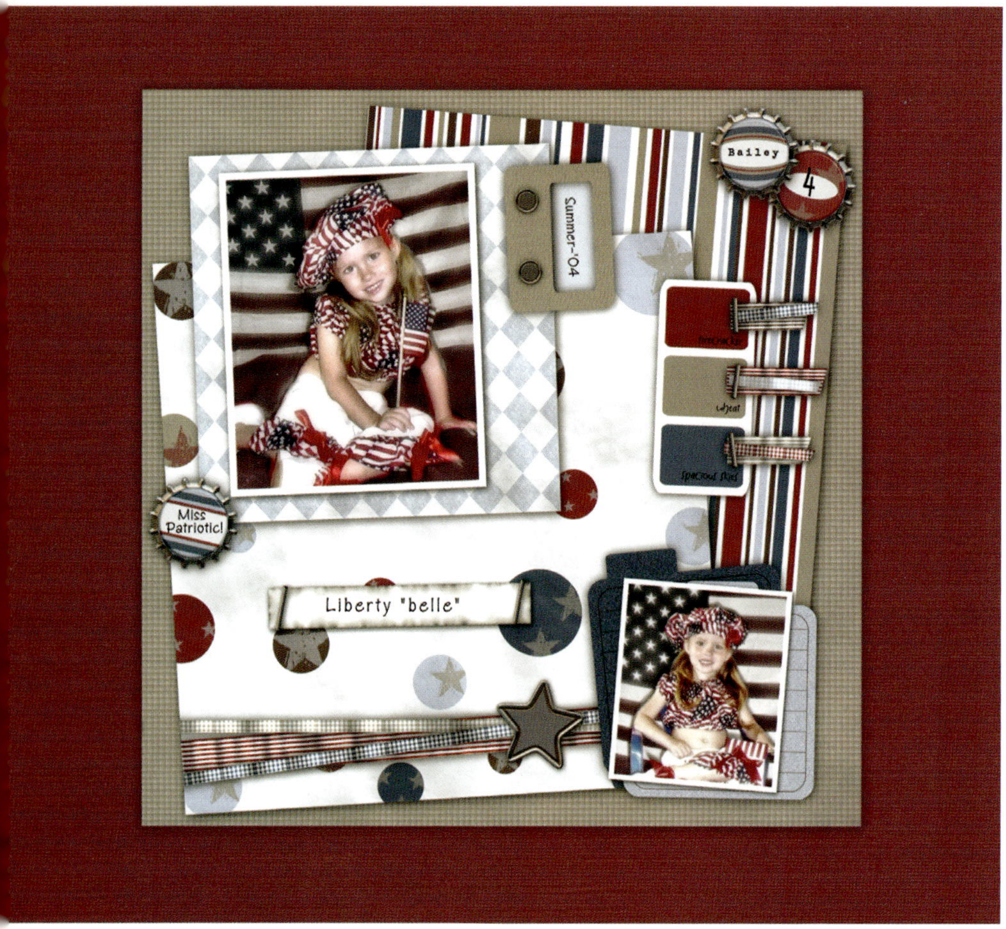

liberty bell

Designer: Michelle Underwood

Layer patterned paper with a computer scrapbooking program. Import photos and mat. Embellish with computer-generated bottle caps, ribbon, paintchip, charm and metal tab.

talon

Designer: Michelle Underwood

Create a digital scrapbooking page with layered patterned paper. Mat imported photos. Embellish with metal embellishments, ribbon, charms and tags.

sweet baby girl

Designer: Michelle Underwood

Use a scrapbooking computer program to create layered paper. Import photos, size and crop. Add title with font to create labeler printed effect. Finish with ribbon, monogram and charm.

computer scrapbooking

Learn a new approach to scrapbooking with the aid of your computer. If you have ever downloaded a new font, you have just made your first step toward digital scrapbooking. Computer scrapbooking programs can be purchased at the scrapbook store. Computer designers have created many layouts; simply add your photos and print. Digital papers, charms, ribbons, brads and assortments of scrapbook techniques can be found on the internet. You may also purchase different digital scrapbooking services. The user-friendly digital designs will help you create amazing layouts.

photo manipulation

bailey

Designer: Michelle Underwood

Generate computer layer paper for a background. Tie ribbon knots, band ribbon across layout and add metal charms. Create title and add aging effect.

lake minature, ne

Designer: Amy Teets

Create a computer generated layout. Layer paper to create background; add title and journaling.

JoAnn ScrapEssentials

friends forever

Designer: Julie Ann Shahin

Enlarge photo, change to black and white, use posterize filter and print; mat onto cardstock. Layer patterned papers to create background. Print journaling on patterned paper and adhere to background.

JoAnn ScrapEssentials

happiness is family

Designer: Julie Ann Shahin

Cut background paper in narrow strips and adhere to cardstock. Create title with patterned paper, rub-ons and stickers. Layer transparency over an altered photo.

autumn

Designer: Sherry Wright

Print a photo on transparency and adhere to patterned paper. Place another photo on top. Tear fabric strip; adhere silk leaves and leaf embellishment.

portrait of love

Designer: Susan Hubbs

Manipulate a photo to look like an artist's sketch; print on patterned cardstock. Create title with rub-on letters; add metal charms, clip and ribbon a layered patterned paper background.

my champion

Designer: Sue Fields

Computer alter and print photo in green. Layer cardstock and photos to create background. Print title on cardstock. Embellish with brads and photo turns.

engagement photo

Designer: NanC & Company

Print photo on textured cardstock; mat and ink edges. Layer cardstock and patterned paper; punch holes, ink, sand and curl patterned paper edge. Embellish with distressed cardstock flowers and brads.

photo manipulation

spin

Designer: Heidi Knight

Open your digital photos and edit using a photo-manipulation software program. Crop and paste all images to "main" photo. Digitally assemble photos into desired layout. Layer highlighing e-papers and embellishments. Add journaling to your layout and drop shadows to your photos and elements.

step 1

Choose a main photo and several other photos of the same person. Select the subjects in other photos using the elliptical marquee. Cut and paste to the main photo. Adjust the size of each layer so that the subjects in the background are smaller than those in the foreground. Erase unwanted areas of each layer using the soft-edged eraser and flatten the layers. Save photo at 300 pixels per inch.

step 2

Open your scrapbooking software. Import manipulated main photo. Insert patterned paper layer to the top and bottom of main photo. Select and insert monogram tag and other e-embellishments.

step 3

Add drop shadows. Then add journaling by selecting the text tool and clicking where you want to begin. Save the layout first as a PhotoShop (PSD) document for editing later. Then save the layout as a JPEG file at a quality of 10 or greater for printing.

JoAnn ScrapEssentials

kelsie

Designer: NanC & Company

Layer cardstock and patterned transparency to create the background. Hand stitch on the background to emphasize pattern. Create title with metal letters; add paper clip and stickers. Sew hidden journaling pocket and tuck inside photo.

JoAnn ScrapEssentials

one in a million

Designer: NanC & Company

Create mini mosaic with photos, paper and square-page pebbles. Layer printed vellum on cardstock for background. Add assorted metal embellishments, stickers and brads.

un tendre calin

Designer: Marie-Eve Bélanger

Print photo in sepia color tones and ink the edges. Create tag pocket in background patterned paper mat. Embellish with tags, ribbon, and metals. Add wooden letters and stickers for title and journaling.

Jo-Ann ScrapEssentials

with a kiss & a dance

Designer: Julie Ann Shahin

Layer patterned paper and stitch; fold paper strips in half and create a paper binding on edges. Use sticker quotes and letters for title and handwrite journaling tag. Embellish with ribbon, flowers, button, brads and safety-pinned fibers. Reduce several photos on computer. Print and mat photos.

photo manipulation

Altering your photographs is a great way to make them look better and add interest to your layout. There are so many ways to alter your photos from changing colors or sizes to printing them on different mediums. Here are some suggestions that will enhance the quality of your photos:

- Use a good quality program such as PhotoShop or Paint Pro
- Use a good quality scanner to scan your photos at a minimum resolution of 300 pixels per square inch
- Spot color to emphasize certain objects
- Restore and enhance the color of old photographs
- Create fuzzy borders
- Add filters for interest and varitey
- Crop photos to focus attention
- Enlarge or reduce to harmonize layout
- Adjust the saturation levels to naturalize or stylize
- Print using various mediums such as textured cardstock, canvas, fabric, watercolor paper, art paper, vellum or transparency paper

Before altering a photo, scan it into the computer; then copy the image as your "working file." Keep the original in your archives so that you will always have access to it. When you are using a computer program to alter your photos, you can save time by putting the toolbar on the desktop so that you have easy access.

road trip

Designer: Pam Callaghan

Print an enlarged photo of a compass head on cardstock; sand and distress with ink. Add compass pointing needle and center to make it look real. Print title and journaling on transparency and cardstock. Adhere to patterned paper. Finish with 3-D embellishments, and stapled fabric strips.

photo manipulation

Jo-Ann ScrapEssentials

tulips

Designer: Janet Schroede

Spot color the tulip. Cut paper into strips and adhere to background. Embellish with chipboard monogram, brads and ribbon. Create title from punched-out patterned paper letters.

Jo-Ann ScrapEssentials

why a scorpio?

Designer: Kelly Goree

Print photos in four tints and adhere to layered patterned paper background. Stitch background to mimic the shapes found on the patterned paper. Handwrite journaling on photo mat. Create title with cardstock stickers. Embellish with bookplate and brads.

it's me

Designer: Cheryl Baase

Create a background of patterned paper and cardstock. Ink layout with white and black inks. Finish with sized-and-matted photos and rub-on letters.

JoAnn ScrapEssentials

simply you

Designer: Julie Ann Shahin

Layer cardstock, sized photos and ribbon to create background. Embellish with felt flowers, buttons and brads. Create title with stamped letters.

Abby, now that you are three, you are full of questions, and WHY is a regular part of your vocabulary.
WHY is that car red?
why is it raining?
WHY do I have to go to bed?
I'll let you in on a little secret: Growing up doesn't mean you'll have all the answers. In fact, now that I'm your Mom, I have some new questions. So, now it's my turn to ask you WHY.
WHY does ketchup make every food more appealing?
WHY are you afraid of your stereo?
why can't you be potty-trained?
WHY DO YOU INSIST ON WEARING YOUR WARMEST WINTER PAJAMAS IN THE MIDDLE OF JULY?
won't you eat any food that has, or has once had, or you think has had, any kind of seeds?
WHY DO YOU ALWAYS ANSWER THE QUESTION "why ARE YOU DOING THAT?" WITH "'CUZ THAT'S why I AM!"
WHY, when you have a whole house full of toys, do you always think the most interesting toy is whatever Micah is playing with?
WHY do all these little things make me love you even more?
As hard as I try to come up with logical (or at least creative) answers to all of your whys and all of my WHYs, perhaps your answer is sometimes best: "Cuz that's WHY!"

Chapter 10

journaling

Pictures say a thousand words but journaling can record memories word for word. There are endless ways to add journaling to your scrapbooks. A variety of methods can liven up your albums. Let your own journaling jar, like the one presented in this section, become a resourse to spawn new and clever ideas for journaling pages when you need inspiration. Participating in a circle journal, like the one that follows, can inspire you to use creative journaling techniques. Capture multiple perspectives on single events by asking family members and friends to journal the same event.

i called you mary

Designer: Sharyn Tormanen

Print journaling on cardstock and patterned paper. Create title with rub-on and sticker letters.

JoAnn ScrapEssentials

life lessons

Designer: Pam Callaghan

Cut circles and a band out of patterned paper; adhere to a cardstock background. Create title with cardstock letter and printed writing. Edit photos and add text with a computer program. Conceal journaling behind tags. Embellish with ribbon and brads.

Jo-Ann ScrapEssentials

inspiration journal jar

Designer: Becky Heisler

Cover a canning jar with patterned paper. Add assorted ribbons, flowers, metal words, tag and stickers. Fill with journaling thoughts to inspire writing.

purr sonalities

Designer: Heather Siebel

Jo-Ann ScrapEssentials

Create layout with patterned paper and cardstock. Conceal journaling in library pocket and mini file folder. Add assorted 3-D acrylic letters, rub-ons and clip.

journaling

Jo-Ann ScrapEssentials

cousins' family journal

Designer: Sam Cousins

Cover a journal with inked patterned paper and cardstock. Embellish with sanded stickers, flower, ribbon knots, monogram, brads and small tag. Tie closed with thick ribbon.

Jo-Ann ScrapEssentials

1st lost tooth

Designer: Michelle Hubbartt

Mat photo on hinged cardstock. Embellish background with eyelets, metal photo corners, twill ribbon, rickrack and chipboard journaling squares. Tuck tooth in memory envelope.

circle journals

Circle journals provide wonderful ways to connect scrapbooking with friendships. These journals are becoming more popular among groups of friends. Together a group can complete an entire journal or album in a short amount of time. Circle journals may have a variety of themes such as recipes, quotes, favorite things, holidays, parties, celebrations, dreams, stories, thoughts and memories. Before getting started, decide who will participate in the group and what the theme will be. The first person creates one or two embellished pages that focus on journaling and then passes their finished pages to the next person until all have contributed. You may use many different kinds of albums to create unique circle journals. Create your own pocket album, tag book or a ribbon-bound chipboard album. To save time, fill a pre-made mini album or a plain-bound sketch book. Once the journal is done, look for a fun way to store it, and it will be a treasured keepsake for years to come.

JoAnn ScrapEssentials

family circle journal

Designer: NanC & Company

Alter a children's book to create a circle journal. Paint pages, fill with patterned paper and hand journaling. Create tabs with cardstock stickers. Embellish journal with stickers, ribbon knots, metal tags and rub-on letters.

journaling

JoAnn ScrapEssentials

the gift

Designer: Cheryl Baase

Print journaling on cardstock, trim, ink and adhere to patterned paper and cardstock. Create title and print on transparency. Mat photo on coordinating paper. Apply ink around the edges of patterneded paper and cardstock. Finish with brads, paper strip, fiber and metal tag.

things i am thankful four

Designer: NanC & Company

JoAnn ScrapEssentials

Divide a composition book into sections with title tabs for easy reference. Embellish cover with patterned paper, stitched ribbon, stamped title, letter stickers, rub-ons and metal accents. Fill journal with matted photos, rub-ons and hand written messages.

diagnosis a reader

Designer: Pam Callaghan

Create a background with a photo border, patterned paper and cardstock. Use a computer to create a "patient chart" and a semi-circle title. Add rub-on letters and stamped image. Finish with ribbon, aging ink, stitching and staples.

calvin khan

Designer: Robin Hohenstern

Print journaling and title on cardstock. Coordinate the title with photo initials. Adhere to layered patterned paper. Embellish with photo, jute and coin.

journaling

JoAnn ScrapEssentials

crocodile tears

Designer: Felicia Krelwitz

Create title with zipper, labeler and mailbox letters. Round corners on the background, cardstock and patterned paper. Ink edges and add stickers, ribbon, clips, acrylic circle and brads.

journaling

A great layout must have journaling to make it complete. Imaginative journaling will highlight special moments and capture the feelings of life's special events. A good way to remember events and moments in your life is to record them in a journal or notebook. That way when you are scrapbooking a page or making an album, you will have access to all sorts of information that will convey feelings of the moment. Keep a small journal tucked into your purse or pocket for easy access or use a journal jar. Just make sure to fill it on a regular basis with topics that can spark your imagination.

There are several ways to journal:

- Create library card pockets to hold journaling tags
- Use assorted fonts and text sizes
- Unify journaling with a single word
- Create titles with initials
- Emphasize journaling words in boxes
- Tell a story
- Create hidden tags
- Conceal journaling hinged photo mat
- Make a list
- Write personal letters
- Tuck love note in a pocket
- Handwrite messages so that your personal writting will be preserved

cute as a button

Designer: Dawn Taranto

Cut patterned paper strips to create background. Create journaling and title with rub-on words and stickers and large button. Embellish with rickrack, flowers, ribbons and jewels.

JoAnn ScrapEssentials

love notes box

Designer: Jill Stenglein

Paint lidded box, sand and ink edges. Tear patterned paper, ink and adhere to lid. Add embellishments, stamp "notes," and place "love" charms between letters. Add ribbon and buckle to box.

journaling

JoAnn ScrapEssentials

life unscripted

Designer: Tracy Clements

Print journaling on cardstock; border background with patterned paper and ribbon. Mat photos and create title with rub-on letters.

JoAnn ScrapEssentials

5 things that make you laugh

Designer: Becky Heisler

Trace and cut number; cover with paper. Cut circle and tear bottom of rectangle. Print, cut and staple journaling strips on to paper. Create title on photo with rub-on letters and words. Embellish with flowers, small tags and fiber.

why?

Designer: Rebekah Bissel

Print journaling on cardstock using a variety of fonts. Highlight a special word using assorted 3-D letters and embellishments.

what say?

Designer: Kay Rogers

Layer patterned paper to create a background and add photo. Punch a row of holes on mat and tie ribbons. Print and mat journaling boxes. Create title with cut-out patterned paper letters.

the time of our lives
hyannisport
There shall be eternal summer in the grateful heart
HONEYMOON
DUCKMOBILE TOUR

Chapter 11

scrapbooking

Scrapbooking is more than just a hobby: it is an art form, a creative outlet, a way to preserve memories, an expression of self. Scrapbooking is as varied as the people that create albums. Notice the many different subjects scrapbooked in this section, ranging from scenery to relationships to travel. Don't limit yourself to doing what has been done. Chart a new course. Who knows, your friends might start copying you.

scrapbooking

me

Designer: Lisa Pace

Adhere photos to a layered patterned paper background with dimensional foam tape. Print journaling, cut into paper strips and ink edges. Punch flowers; add knotted buttons and hand journaling. Embellish with labeler stickers.

forever

Designer: Heidi Deck

Create background with sewn patterned paper and cardstock. Attach ribbon and brads along seam. Print photo on canvas, ink the mat edges and add metal letter charms. Add journaling, brads, metal charms and ribbon.

katie

Designer: NanC & Company

Layer cardstock and patterned paper to create background. Ink and sand the edges. Hand stitch swirls. Add assorted brads, stickers, stapled ribbon and photos corners. Create title with rub-on letters.

natural beauty

Designer: Lily Goldsmith

Layer patterned paper and adhere to background. Distress chipboard letters with ink. Staple ribbon across layout and add rub-on letters. Create a collage with flower, bookplate and mesh.

Jo-Ann ScrapEssentials

chinese garden

Designer: Sandra Helder

Stitch patterned paper, cardstock and matted photos. Embellish with tag, coin charm, photo turns and metal letters.

Jo-Ann ScrapEssentials

the streets of paris

Designer: Susan Stringfellow

Stamp diamond image on a cardstock background with heated embossing powder. Chalk background randomly. Stitch background with a decorative sewing machine stitch. Adhere matted photos, tags, diecut and photo corners. Stamp and print journaling.

london guard

Designer: Leisa Tobler

Jo-Ann ScrapEssentials

Enlarge photo, print and mat. Create title with inked stickers. Embellish with bookplate, tags, brads and fiber.

Jo-Ann ScrapEssentials

hyannis port

Designer: Julie Ann Shahin

Tear fabric strip and adhere over background patterned paper and photo background. Tear vellum and staple to corner. Frame key in leather frame; add metal tags and sticker letters.

scrapbooking

a winning hand

Designer: Felicia Krelwitz

Create title and initial with rub-on letters. Use round corner punch on photo and paper. Embellish with ribbons, brad, flowers, bottle cap and playing cards.

Jo-Ann ScrapEssentials

sole mates

Designer: Felicia Krelwitz

Layer assorted patterned paper onto cardstock and ink edges. Create title with chipboard and rub-on letters. Embellish with ribbon, tag flower and journaling.

JoAnn ScrapEssentials

honoring those that served

Designer: Tristann Graves

Arrange matted photos and tags on cardstock background. Create title and journaling with printed transparency; add metal charms.

JoAnn ScrapEssentials

drew

Designer: NanC & Company

Create a background from strips of cardstock; sand the edges. Cut monogram from cardstock, mat and adhere with adhesive foam dot. Finish with brads, rub-on letters and 3-D embellishment.

got wheels?

Designer: Deborah Hodge

Create the background from layered patterned paper. Add journaling printed onto cardstock, staples, ribbon, buttons, brads, letters and photo turns. Ink tracks and shapes on paper.

step 1

Cut different sizes of black strips out of cardstock and adhere to patterned paper. Mat onto cardstock background.

step 2

Print journaling on cardstock. Layer patterned paper strips and adhere to background with staples. Ink toy car tires and roll or stamp on background paper. Adhere ribbon to edges of patterned paper.

step 3

Mat photos on cardstock and adhere to background. Adhere chipboard washers with color brads in the center.

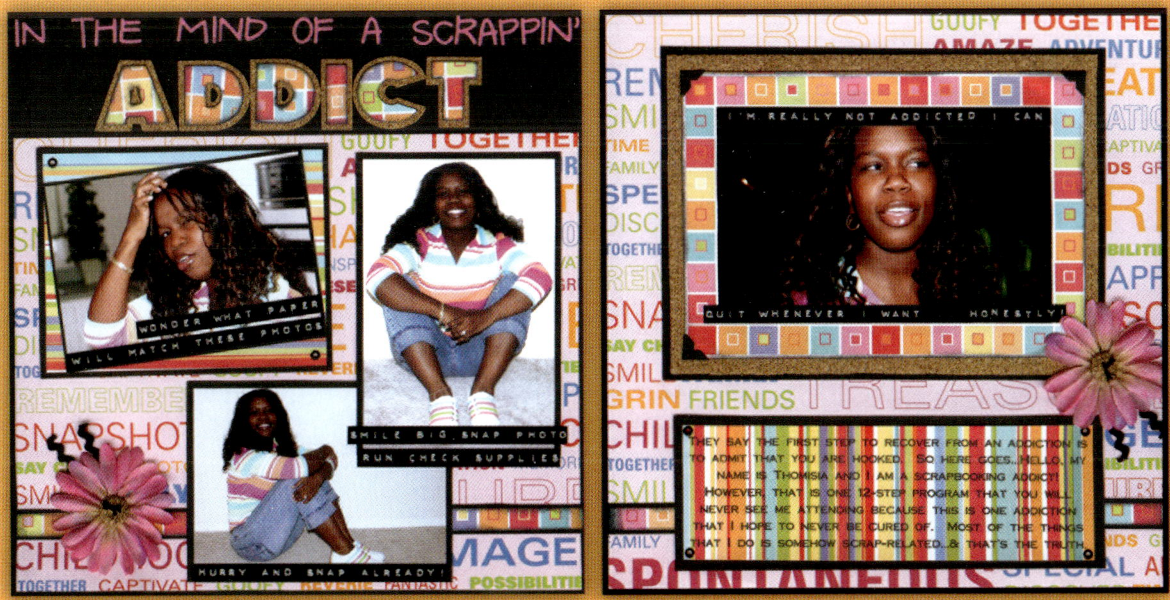

addict

Designer: Thomisia Francois

Layer patterned paper and cardstock for background; attach matted photos. Create title with stickers, patterned paper and cork letters. Print journaling on matted patterned paper. Create additional journaling and title with labeler-printed stickers. Add silk flowers with cork button.

Jo-Ann ScrapEssentials

a grand obsession

Designer: Kayla Richards

Create background by layering patterned paper on cardstock. Staple ribbon loops; add flowers with brad centers. Print journaling on cardstock, ink edges and add rub-on letters.

JoAnn ScrapEssentials

major intensity

Designer: Sara Bryans

Print enlarged photo and mat on patterned paper. Create title with metal letters and rub-on words. Finish with brads, metal tag and fiber.

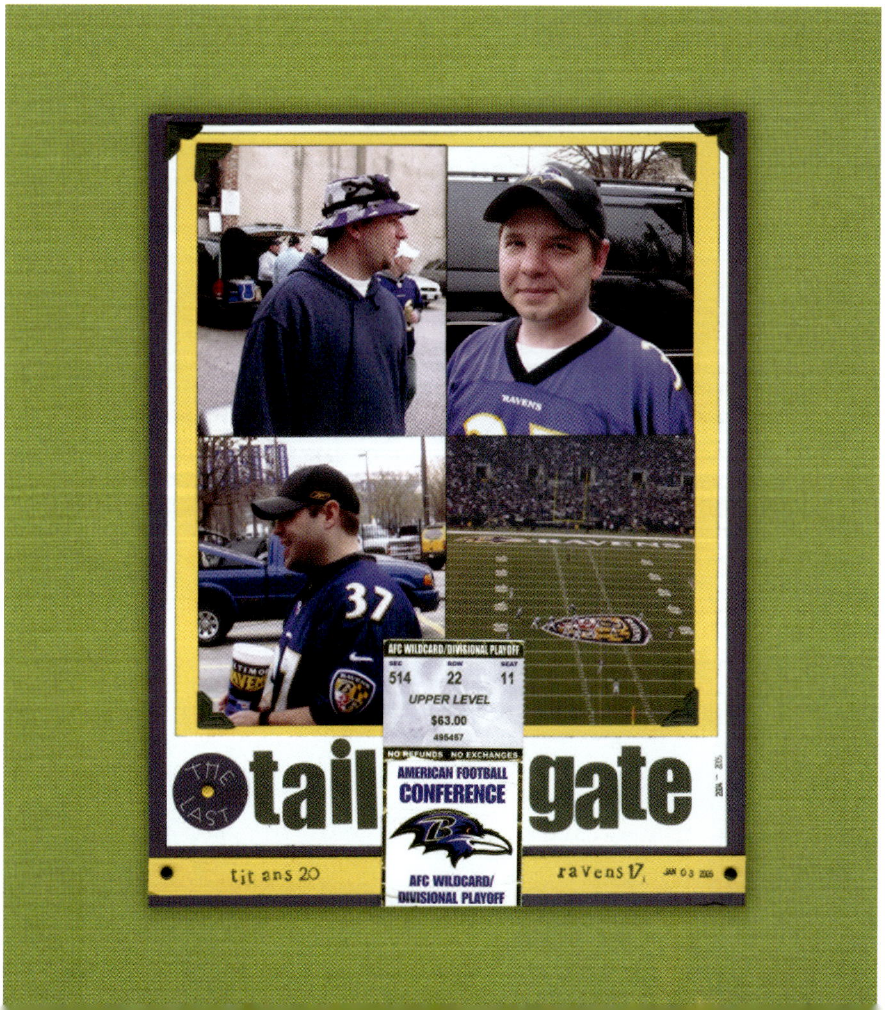

JoAnn ScrapEssentials

the last tailgate

Designer: Cheryl Rohe

Create a background with layered cardstock. Create title with rub-on and sticker letters. Stamp journaling; add photo corners and ticket.

my hero

Designer: Maria Burke

Create background with patterned paper. Print journaling on to cardstock blocks. Staple vellum quote and attach snaps.

Jo-Ann ScrapEssentials

volleyball

Designer: Kay Rogers

Paint on the reverse side of transparency title and adhere to patterned paper. Double mat photos; add stickers and label journaling. Embellish with ribbon metal washer, tags, photo turns and ribbon.

scrapbooking

souvenirs d'une vie

Designer: Marie-Eve Bélanger

Fill patterned paper background with assorted mini albums and pockets. Create title and journaling with stickers. Add 3-D embellishments, flowers, tags and fiber.

You are my everything

Designer: Pam Callaghan

Stitch heart-shaped cardstock band to patterned paper background; tie ribbon knots. Create title with rub-on letters. Attach metal charm and tags.

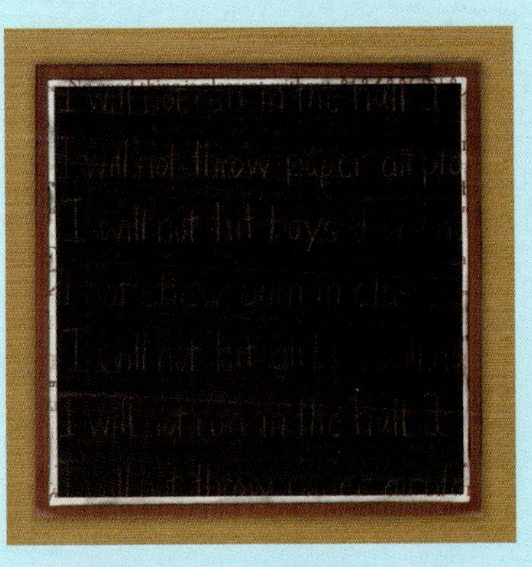

step 1

Layer patterned paper and cardstock to create background; ink the edges.

step 2

Print one of the photos in black and white. Mat photos with inked cardstock. Attach paperclip to one of the photos and adhere to background.

step 3

Make a scroll embellishment with rolled paper and a key tied with ribbon. Place a metallic tag quote on the page. Create title with stamped ribbon and adhere to background.

Jo-Ann ScrapEssentials

college bound

Designer: NanC & Company

Create a page with layered patterned paper and cardstock; ink the edges. Embellish with altered photo, handmade embellishment, ribbon and definition.

JoAnn ScrapEssentials

now & then

Designer: NanC & Company

Layer patterned paper on cardstock and stitch to create background. Print journaling on cardstock; crumple and ink surface. Add ribbon, metal charms and embellished tag. Create title with sticker letters and numbers.

JoAnn ScrapEssentials

you

Designer: Lily Goldsmith

Create block background with photo, patterned paper and transparency. Embellish with letters, ribbon, stickers, brads and fabric labels. Add color to chipboard letters with ink.

JoAnn ScrapEssentials

love always

Designer: Tistann Graves

Print photo with halo edge; overlap with printed transparencies, patterned paper and cardstock. Embellish with metal tags and ribbon.

JoAnn ScrapEssentials

new beginnings

Designer: Julie Ann Shahin

Overlap patterned paper strip on photo. Print journaling quote on cardstock background. Use rub-on words for title. Finish with ribbon, acrylic letters, definition tag and brad.

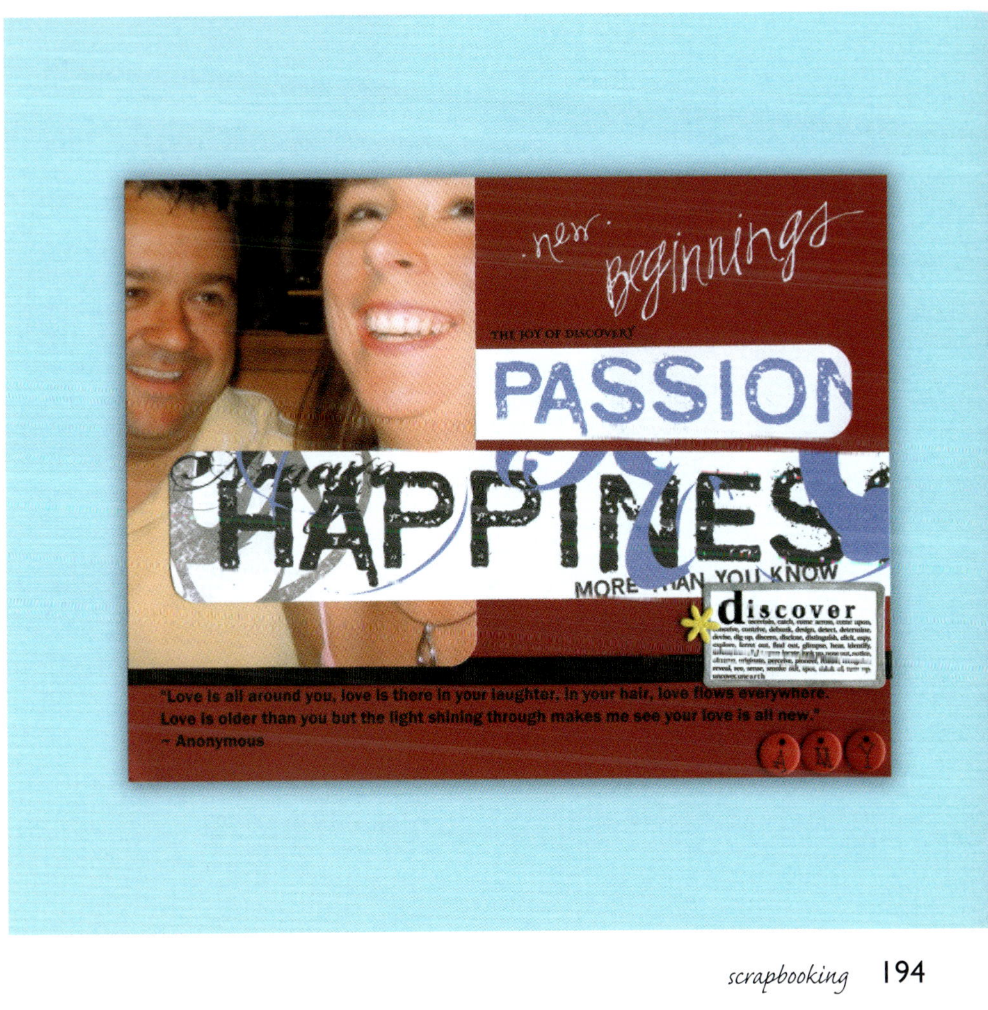

supplies

Key:

AC	American Crafts
BG	BasicGrey
BZ	Bazzill
CB	Chatterbox
CI	Creative Imaginations
DCWV	Diecuts With a View
HS	Heidi Swapp
JAE	JoAnn ScrapEssentials
JA	JoAnn Fabric's Products
LD	Li'l Davis
MM	Making Memories

gift ideas

grandpa's adventure box
Cardstock: DCWV
Patterned Paper: DCWV
Fabric Letters: JAE
Corkboard Letters: CI
Turquoise Letters: JAE
Blue Letter: JAE
Rub-on's: JAE
Clear Tile Letter: JAE
Ribbon: DCWV
Box of Cards: DCWV
Brads: DCWV
Cork Letter: JAE
Page Pebble: JAE
Alphabet Stickers: DCWV, Memories in the Making

party girl clipboard
Patterned Paper: Gin X
Ribbon: JAE
Acrylic Word: JAE
Metal Word: JAE
Envelope: JAE
Rub-on: JAE
Ink: Tim Holtz

angie's address book
Cardstock: DCWV
Patterned Paper: DCWV
Appliqué: JAE
Bookplate: JAE
Brads: JAE
Flowers: Prima
Ribbon: Fibers by the Yard
Stamps: Hero Arts

sunburn first aid kit
Patterned Paper: Target
First Aid Kit: Target
Bottle Cap: LD
Diecut: DCWV
Fiber: www.fbty.com
Metal Charm: JAE
Font: 2peas Mr. Giggles
Transparency: Staples

daisy luggage tag
Cardstock: DCWV
Ribbon: Maya Road
Rub-ons: MM
Luggage Tag: 3M
Daisy Punch: EK Success
Circle Punch: EK Success

grandmommy's brag book
Patterned Paper: BG
Metal Clip Letters: JAE
Chipboard Letter: LD
Rub-ons: MM, Hudson Card Embellishments
Charm: Hudson Card Embellishments
Flower: HS
Ribbon: MM, Hudson Card Embellishments
Ribbon Slide Letters: MM

through the years
Cardstock: DCWV
Patterned Paper: DCWV
Rub-ons: K&Company
Brads: JAE
Ribbon: May Arts
Stickers: JAE
Vellum Quote: DCWV
Stamps: PSX
Metal Tag: MM

apple recipe box
Patterned Paper: DCWV
Bookplate: JAE
Brads: JAE
Ink: JAE
Box: JA
Ribbon: Fibers by the Yard
Pom-pom Trim: JA
Stamps: Rubber Stamp Ave, Close to My Heart
Paint: Plaid

notes for miss massey
Cardstock: DCWV
Wood: JA
Rub-ons: JAE, MAMBI
Metal Clip: MM
Ribbon: JA
Stamp: Capress Stamps
3-D Stickers: JAE

true friends
Cardstock: DCWV
Patterned Paper: DCWV
Ribbon: Offray
Photo Holders: JAE
Brads: JAE
Safety Pins: JAE
Rub-on: DCWV

inspirational tag book
Tags: DCWV & SEI
Vellum Quotes: DCWV
Brads: SEI
Ribbon: SEI
Stickers: SEI
Rub-ons: SEI

flower coaster set
Cardstock: DCWV
Patterned Paper: DCWV
Bookplate: JAE
Ribbon: Offray

dad glass frame
Cardstock: DCWV
Overlay: DCWV

plexi-glass coaster
Cardstock: DCWV
Patterned Paper: DCWV
Rub-ons: DCWV
Alphabet Stickers: DCWV
Ribbon: JAE

mini file folder album
Cardstock: DCWV
Patterned Paper: Sweetwater
Transparency: Sweetwater
Buttons: Junkitz
Metal Frame: K&Company
Word Stick Pin: JAE
Bookplate: JAE
Ink: Clearsnap
Brads: JAE
Staples: MM
Rub-on: JAE
Flower: Prima
Safety Pins: JAE

my teacher thank you gift
Patterned Paper: DCWV
Stickers: DCWV
Metal Tag: JAE
Bubble Accent: JAE
Fabric: JA
Candle: JA
Ink: Ranger

family birthdays album
Cardstock: BZ
Patterned Paper: Daisy D's
Book: HS
Ribbon: MM, May Arts
Rub-ons: MM
Tag: JAE
Charms: Memories in the Making
Ink: Fluid Chalk

altered apple recipe tin
Cardstock: DCWV
Patterned Paper: DCWV, Colorbok, HOTP, Me & My Big Ideas
Stamp: Stampin' Up, Scrabble, CI
Ink: StazOn

birthday bag
Cardstock: DCWV
Patterned Paper: DCWV
Ribbon: MM, AC
Alphabet Stickers: DCWV

monogram birthday invitation
Cardstock: DCWV
Patterned Paper: DCWV
Ribbon: AC, DCWV

pink purse
Cardstock: DCWV
Eyelets: JAE
Brads: JAE
Texture Plates: Fiskars
Texture Tool: Fiskars

albums

boy mini album
Patterned Paper: DCWV
Rub-ons: DCWV, JAE
Clips: JAE
Brads: JAE
Ribbon: JAE
Fabric Stickers: JAE
Stamps: Provo Craft, MM
Ink: Tim Holtz
Flowers: Prima

portland trip album
Patterned Paper: BG
Album: DCWV
Ribbon: May Arts, Doodle Bug
Brads: MM
Stamp: Dingbats

Metal Tag: BG, CI
Chipboard Letters: LD
Alphabet Stickers: BG

a new start...life in rescue
Cardstock: BZ
Patterned Paper: CB, Karen Foster
Word Tag: CB
Stickers: Pebbles, EK Success, AMM
Brads: JAE, CB
Fibers: JAE, CB
Metal Charms: JAE
Ink: Van Dyke

senior pictures album
Patterned Paper: Bo-Bunny
Ribbon: May Arts, CI
Chipboard Numbers: LD
Plastic Tag: CI
Metal Letter: JAE
Word Embellishment: JAE
Stickers: Autumn Leaves
Metal Embellishments: K&Company, BG, 7 Gypsies
Wooden Embellishments: K&Company, BG

altered purse accordion album
Patterned Paper: JAE
Stickers: JAE, MM
Metal Alpha Clips: JAE
Ribbon: Textured Trios
Wooden Purse: Wal-Mart
Ink: Ranger
Stamps: PSX

home circle journal
Cardstock: Archivers
Patterned Paper: Rusty Pickle, DCWV
Paintchips: Club Scrap
Circle Clips: MM
Eyelet Numbers: MM
Photo Corner: MM
Tags: MM
Metal Plaque: MM
Ribbon Charm: MM
Rub-ons: MM
Photo Anchor: MM
Brads: MM
Zipper Pull: All My Memories
Ribbon: May Arts
Ink: Memories
Clip: 7 Gypsies

my summer trip album
Cardstock: DCWV
Stamps: CI
Rub-ons: JAE, Scrapworks
Ribbon: AC
Acrylic Word: JAE
Black Letters: JAE
Metal Letters: JAE

lake ontario paper bag album
Patterned Paper: Sassafrass Lass
Bookplate: JAE
Alphabet Stickers: MM
Brad: MM
Stickers: Karen Foster, Shotz by Danelle Johnson
Rub-ons: Provo Craft, Royal Brush, Sandy Lion
Ink: Colorbox

bailey's book
Patterned Paper: DCWV
Album: DCWV
Metallic Bookplates: DCWV
Saying Sticker: DCWV
Ribbon: JAE, AC, MM
Brads: JAE
Alphabet Stickers: DCWV
Word Stickers: DCWV
Metallic Word: DCWV
Paintchips: Behr

weight loss diary
Cardstock: BZ
Chipboard Letters: HS
Jewels: HS
Rub-ons: HS
Chipboard Strips: HS
Chipboard Shapes: HS
Flower: Prima
Paint: MM
Ink: Ranger
Ribbon: JA

my trip to disneyland accordion album
Cardstock: DCWV
Patterned Paper:
Cork Letters: CI
Alphabet Stickers: DCWV
Ribbon: AC, DCWV
Bookplate: DCWV
Paintchips: Behr
Brads: JAE, DCWV
Fibers: JAE

nana's brag book
Cardstock: DCWV
Patterned Paper: DCWV
Cork Letters: JAE
Brads: DCWV
Flowers: Prima
Metal Letter: JAE

photo shoot album
Cardstock: DCWV, BZ
Patterned Paper: CB
Album: DCWV
Rub-ons: MM
Brads: MM, JAE
Photo Corner: MM
Flowers: JA
Stickers: CI, CB, Rusty Pickle
Wooden Letter: LD
Ribbon: May Arts, MM
Ink: Colorbox

family score book
Cardstock: DCWV
Patterned Paper: Paper Love, DCWV
Rub-ons: JAE
Labels: JA
Alphabet Stickers: MM
Acrylic Words: JAE
Ribbon: AC, MM
Leather Frame: JAE

childhood memories album
Chipboard Frame: HS
Album: CR Gibson
Rub-ons: Kelly Panacei
Flowers: Prima
Glaze: Judikins
Word Tiles: JAE
Alphabet Stickers: Pebbles Inc.
Ribbon: DCWV

july vacation matchbook album
Album: Memories in the Making
Metal Plate: Memories in the Making

cousins paintchip mini album
Cardstock: DCWV
Patterned Paper: DCWV
Bookplates: JAE
Page Pebble: JAE
Monogram Sticker: DCWV
Photo Holders: JAE
Sticker: JAE
Brads: JAE
Ribbon: DCWV
Rub-ons: DCWV, JAE

love album
Patterned Paper: Autumn Leaves, CB Inc, 7 Gypsies, Paper Reflections, Anna Griffin, K&Company, Pebbles
Alphabet Stickers: LD
Stickers: DCWV, Bo Bunny Press, Pebbles, MM

kids

a flower for mom
Patterned Paper: LD
Stamps: PSX
Stencil: Rusty Pickle
Stickers: Doodle Bug
Brads: JAE
Flowers: JAE
Belt Buckle: JAE
Book Plate: Carolee's

precious julia
Cardstock: BZ
Alphabet Stickers: LD
Ink: Colorbox
Ribbon: MM
Flowers: MM
Clip: Rebecca Sower
Stamps: Leave Memories

bubbles are my favorite things
Cardstock: BZ
Patterned Paper: BG, SEI
Eyelets: MM
Ribbon: JA, SEI
Bubbles: Heidi Grace
Circle Clips: Blue Boxer
Tag: Blue Boxer
Straws: Publix
Circle Ring: Office Depot
Stencil Letters: Office Depot
Paint: MM
Rub-ons: MM
Staples: MM
Silver Letters: MM
Brads: MM
Buttons: BZ, SEI
Mesh: Magic Mesh
Tab Letters: Scrapworks
Tabs: Scrapworks
Washers: Lowe's

bill, bugs & ed
Patterned Paper: CB
Ribbon: LD, Close to my Heart
Button: MM
Tag: CB
Fonts: Arial, Pharmacy
Photo Corners: CB
Rivets: CB
Brad: JAE

strong willed
Patterned Paper: Junkitz
Alphabet Stickers: AC, Pebbles
Brads: JAE
Button: JAE
Ribbon: AC
Candy Embellishment: JAE
Fonts: Angelina, Artistamp

abby goes to gymboree
Patterned Paper: BG
Brads: JAE, Architexture
Wood Dominos: JAE
Book plates: JAE
Alphabet Stickers: Provo Craft
Monogram: BG
Leather Flower: MM
Ink: Tim Holtz

love to swim
Cardstock: BZ
Patterned Paper: My Mind's Eye
Coasters: My Mind's Eye

live, laugh
Patterned Paper: BG
Stickers: BG, CI
Tag: BG
Buttons: SEI
Transparency: CI
Film Strip: CI
Fibers: JAE

my boys
Cardstock: DCWV
Alphabet Stickers: Me & My Big Ideas, JAE
Ribbon: Offray
Rub-ons: Me & My Big Ideas
Screws: JAE
Sticker Quote: DCWV

the braves 2005 season
Patterned Paper: Art Warehouse
Epoxy: CI
Transparency: Daisy D's
Stickers: 7 Gypsies
Blue Words: MM

love & be loved
Cardstock: Paper Reflections
Patterned Paper: Fancy Pants
Ribbon: Offray, Wild Asparagus
Fabric: MM
Vellum Quote: DCWV
Key: JAE
Stickers: Fancy Pants
Font: Problem Secretary

life
Patterned Paper: MM
Fabric: JA
Metal Plaque: MM
Rub-ons: MM
Bug Charms: JAE
Hinge: MM
Button: MM
Brads: MM
Book Plate: MM

typical ford
Patterned Paper: JAE, DCWV
Ribbon: Offray
Alphabet Stickers: JAE, AC
Ink: Versacolor
Brads: JAE
Rub-ons: JAE
Fonts: Californian FB, Creampuff

boucherville
Patterned Paper: BG
Wooden Letters: Dollarama
Paint: DecoArt
Rub-ons: Bobarbo
Stamps: Fontwerk
Ink: Colorbox
Wooden Frame: CB
Alphabet Stickers: BG
Clip: Rebecca Sower

loving 3
Cardstock: DCWV
Patterned Paper: DCWV, CB
Brads: JAE
Rub-ons: HS
Chipboard: HS
Flowers: Prima
Metal letters: MM
Paint: Americana

the dance
Cardstock: BZ
Patterned Paper: Carolees, Kelly Panaci, Autumn Leaves
Ribbon: JAE, Michaels
Rub-ons: JAE
Flowers: JAE
Crystals: Darice
Ink: Color Box
Fasteners: MM
Brads: MM
Font: Papyrus

imagine
Cardstock: BZ
Patterned Paper: Melissa Frances
Rub-ons: Dees, Doodlebug, CI
Ribbon: AC
Quote Sticker: Autumn Leaves

dancers
Cardstock: BZ
Patterned Paper: KI Memories
Flowers: JAE
Ribbon: Offray
Alphabet Stickers: KI Memories

what i love about having a girl
Cardstock: BZ
Patterned Paper: Designs by Reminisce
Brads: MM
Paint: MM
Ribbon: MM
Ink: Ranger
Flower: Jolee's
Metal Embellishments: MM

she wants 2 be a rock star
Patterned Paper: CB, Paperbilities
Decorative Paper: CB
Ink: SU
Fonts: Buddy, GiGi, Kathleen, 2P Blocks Heartfelt, 2P Blocks Little Words, 2P Blocks Music

4th grade
Cardstock: BG
Patterned Paper: BG
Wooden Letters: LD
Alphabet Stickers: MM
Stickers: MM
Frame: MM
"4th": Autumn Leaves

unbearable frustrations of being 3
Patterned Paper: Pages Press, Pebbles in my Pocket
Transparency: K&Company
Stamps: MM
Ink: Vintage
Alphabet Stickers: Pebbles, Bo-Bunny
Metal Letters: JAE
Paint: Plaid
Font: Packard Antique

beauty in a red dress
Cardstock: Paper Accents
Patterned Paper: BG
Ribbon: JAE
Brads: JAE
Rub-ons: JAE
Metal Tag: JAE
Flowers: JAE
Font: Chemistry
Ink: Tim Holtz Distress Ink
Book Darts: CI
Stamps: Hero Arts, Meandcarrielou.com
Chipboard: BZ

a year in the life
Cardstock: DCWV
Metal Letter: MM
Bookplate: JAE
Brads: MM
Eyelets: Close to my Heart
Ribbon: LD, Close to My Heart
Flower: Prima
Jump Ring: MM
Chipboard: LD
Fonts: Arial, Pharmacy

petit pianiste
Patterned Paper: 7 Gypsies, Rusty Pickle
Alphabet Stickers: BG
Ink: Colorbox
Brads: MM, JAE
Bookplate: MM
Tab: Melissa France

delight in the journey
Cardstock: BZ
Patterned Paper: DCWV
Rub-ons: MM
Transparency: MM
Alphabet Stickers: Provo Craft

heritage park
Patterned Paper: Scrap Ease
Mesh: Magenta Maruyama
Sticker Quote: Wordsworth
Ink: Colourbox, Vivid
Fabric Paint: Plaid
Stamp: Stampabilities, PSX
Embossing Powder: Stampendous
Watch Brad: 7 Gypsies
Metal Words: MM
Font: Packard Antique

art by ben
Cardstock: DCWV
Patterned Paper: DCWV
Ribbon: JAE
Composition Book: Target
Rub-on: JAE

my family 2005
Cardstock: DCWV
Overlay: DCWV
Corkboard Letters: JAE
Cork Alphabet: CI

boy shadow box
Patterned Paper: DCWV
Metal Mesh: MM
Paint: MM
Tab: JAE
Alphabet Stickers: Provo Craft, AC

baby photo keepsake box
Fabric Label: JAE
Letter Button: JAE
Decorative Brads: MM

wonder
Patterned Paper: DCWV, Me & My Big Ideas, K&Company, Pebbles
Vellum Quote: DCWV
Diecut Letter: DCWV
Alphabet Stickers: Wordsworth
Stickers: Bo Bunny Press
Brads: Lost Art Treasures
Photo Corner: DCWV

making the cut
Cardstock: BZ
Patterned Paper: Daisy D's
Ribbon: Offray
Metal Clip: JAE
Eyelets: JAE
Envelope: JAE
Foam Stamps: MM
Paint: MM

love
Cardstock: KI, BZ
Patterned Paper: KI
Brads: JAE

one year
Cardstock: BZ
Patterned Paper: Wild Asparagus
Stitching Rub-ons: My Minds Eye
Alphabet Stickers: AC, CI
Flowers: MM
Brads: JAE
Font: Times New Roman

love is the beauty of the soul
Cardstock: DCWV
Patterned Paper: DCWV
Rub-ons: DCWV
Metal Letter: JAE
Metal Embellishment: JAE
Ribbon: Venus Industries
Sticker: Kelly Panaci
Ink: Ranger
Brads: JAE

this thing called love
Cardstock: BZ
Patterned Paper: Rusty Pickle
Ribbon: Boxer
Vellum Quote: MM
Rub-ons: MM
Brad: MM
Ink: Vandyke

beauty
Patterned Paper: Wild Asparagus, K&Company, Daisy D's
Brads: JAE
Ribbon: Offray
Tag: Melissa France
Rub-ons: CB
Font: Ancient Script

wedding

wedding invitation
Cardstock: DCWV
Patterned Paper: Mari-Mari
Jewels: JAE

wedding thank you card
Cardstock: DCWV
Patterned Paper: Mari-Mari
Ribbon: DCWV, Offray
Metal Tag: JAE
Rub-on: JAE
Ribbon Tape: Creating Keepsakes

wedding notebook
Cardstock: DCWV
Patterned Paper: Mari-Mari
Buttons: MM
Fabric Flower: JAE
Ribbon: DCWV, Offray
Metal Heart: JAE?
Monogram: DCWV
3-D Alphabet Stickers: JAE

wedding program
Cardstock: DCWV
Patterned Paper: Mari-Mari
Metal Tag: JAE
Ribbon: DCWV
Rub-on: JAE

floral center piece
Patterned Paper: DCWV
Ribbon: Offray
Flowers: Mulberry Paper
Metal Letter: JAE

love hanger
Cardstock: DCWV
Patterned Paper: DCWV
Cork Board: Wal-Mart
Ribbon: DCWV, AC
Brads: JAE
Metal Key: JAE
Rub-ons: JAE, MM
Cork Letters: JAE

what i love is near at hand
Cardstock: DCWV
Metal Frame: JAE
Metal Key: JAE
Fold Out Book: Memories in the Making
Acrylic Word: JAE
Word Stick Pin: Nostalgiques
Brads: JAE
Photo Corners: JAE
Vellum Quote: JAE

Clear Quote Stickers: JAE, DCWV
Ribbon: AC, DCWV, Kirkland Signature
Rub-ons: Me & My Big Ideas
Spiral Clip: JAE

party favor suckers
Stickers: JAE
Ribbon: JAE, Offray
Brads: JAE

wedding favor basket
Cardstock: DCWV
Patterned Paper: DCWV
Stickers: JAE

wedding keepsake box
Patterned Paper: DCWV
Metal Words: JAE
Brads: JAE
Clear Sticker Quotes: JAE

wedding vase
Cardstock: DCWV
Ribbon: JAE

unconditional love
Cardstock: BZ
Patterned Paper: Carolee's Creations
Book Plate: JAE
Alphabet Stickers: Sticko
Font: Script MT Bold

table numbers
Cardstock: DCWV, BZ
Patterned Paper: Junkitz, DCWV
Ribbon: May Arts
Brad: JAE

once in a lifetime
Patterned Paper: Junkitz
Tags: 7 Gypsies
Gem Brads: JAE
Rub-ons: JAE, MM, MME
Inspirational Words: JAE
Twill: Junkitz
Stamp: HS
Acrylic Words: JAE

congratulations tag card
Cardstock: DCWV
Patterned Paper: DCWV
Ribbon: AC, DCWV, Offray
Quote: DCWV Reference Book
Brads: JAE
Metal Embellishment: JAE
Flower: Prima
Metallic Words: MM

a charmed life
Cardstock: BZ
Patterned Paper: Wild Asparagus
Brads: MM
Rub-ons: MM
Flowers: Prima
Metal Charm: Prima
Ink: ColoBox
Ribbon: May Arts

celebrate
Cardstock: Paper Company
Patterned Paper: Anna Griffin
Transparency: Karen Russell Narratives
Rhinestones: JAE
Metal Tag: JAE
Metal Word: MM
Ribbon: Offray

wedding candle
Patterned Paper: BZ, DCWV
Ribbon: Offray
Brads: JAE

our love will never fade
Cardstock: DCWV
Metal Tag: JAE
Ribbon: AC
Photo Holders: JAE
Metallic Word Plates: DCWV
Alphabet Stickers: DCWV
Rub-ons: DCWV, MM
Brads: JAE
Metal Photo Holder: JAE

bride
Cardstock: www.scrapartist.com
Patterned Paper: www.scrapbook-elements.com
Ribbon: www.scrapbook-elements.com
Charm: www.scrapbook-element.com
Font: Beautiful, Times

together
Cardstock: DCWV
Patterned Paper: DCWV
Gems: JAE
Close Pin: JAE
Ribbon: AC
Clear Sticker Quote: DCWV
Paintchip: Home Depot

wedding cards box
Patterned Paper: DCWV
Brads: JAE

cherish bride
Patterned Paper: BG, Gin-X
Flowers: JAE
Word Strips: JAE
Rub on: JAE
Alphabet Stickers: Provo Craft,

family
Cardstock: BZ
Patterned Paper: BG
Brads: JAE
Word Plate: JAE
Flowers: Michaels
Fonts: Baramond, Texas Hero
Overlay: Rhonna Farrer July Digital Kit

father of the bride
Cardstock: BZ
Patterned Paper: Reminisce
Ribbon: May Arts
Sticker: K&Company

Cards

friendship card
Cardstock: DCWV
Patterned Paper: DCWV
Brad: JAE
Alphabet Stickers: Two Busy Moms
Clear Frame: MM

fabric card
Cardstock: BZ
Fabric: JA
Fibers: JAE
Stamp: JA
Ink: StazOn

p&k always
Cardstock: DCWV, BZ
Patterned Paper: DCWV
Letters: JAE
Ribbon: AC, BZ
Rub-ons: MM
Brad: MM
Ink: Ranger

u r one in a million
Cardstock: DCWV
Patterned paper: DCWV
Ribbon: DCWV
Page Pebble: JAE
Rub-on: DCWV
Monogram: DCWV
Alphabet Sticker: Memories in the Making

baby boy tin
Patterned Paper: DCWV
Buttons: DCWV
Ribbon: Offray
Acrylic Words: JAE
Rub-ons: DCWV
Paint: Delta

summer card
Cardstock: DCWV, BZ
Patterned Paper: DCWV
Rub-ons: MM
Sticker: AC
Brad: JAE

birthday wish
Cardstock: BZ
Patterned Paper: AC
Brads: JAE
Rub-on: DCWV

hey love card
Cardstock: DCWV
Patterned Paper: DCWV
Metal Word: MM
Buttons: DCWV
Ribbon: DCWV
Rub-ons: DCWV

love you tag
Patterned Paper: KI Memories, Scenic Route, BG
Alphabet Stickers: CB
Rub-on: Doodlebug
Flowers: MM
Brads: JAE
Ribbon: May Arts

baby card
Patterned Paper: Pebbles
Buttons: CI
Bookplate: JAE
Alphabet Stickers: Memories in the Making
Brads: JAE

friends card
Cardstock: BZ, DCWV
Patterned paper: Autumn Leaves
Ribbon: JA
Fibers: EK Success, DMC
Ink: Colorbox
Brads: JAE
Rub-ons: JAE

the magic of christmas
Cardstock: BZ
Patterned Paper: Rustic Diamonds, Bo-Bunny Press
Rub-ons: Provo Craft, Deja Views, Wonderful Words, Holiday Joy
Ink: Colorbox
Brad: Creative Impressions

fabric pocket & tag
Fabric: www.scrapbookfabric.com
Stickers: DCWV
Ribbon: Doodlebug
Brads: JAE
Staples: MM

let it snow
Cardstock: DCWV, BZ
Chalk: Inkadinkadoo

snowflake card
Cardstock: DCWV
Patterned Paper: DCWV
Wooden Ornament: Wal-Mart
Metal Charm: JAE
Ribbon: Fibers by the Yard
Brad: JAE
Paint: MM
Metal Trim: AMACO

christmas card
Cardstock: DCWV
Patterned Paper: DCWV
Metal Charm: JAE
Page Pebble: JAE

may your holidays be filled
Cardstock: DCWV
Envelope Seals: JAE
Card: DCWV
Page Pebbles: JAE
Stickers: DCWV
Brads: DCWV

smile card
Patterned Paper: DCWV
Card: DCWV
Fibers: Offray
Ribbon: Offray
Metal Word: JAE

christmas tag & sleeve
Cardstock: DCWV
Patterned Paper: DCWV
Metal Tag: JAE
Alphabet Sticker: Memories in the Making
Stickers: Memories in the Making
Ribbons: Offray
Fibers: JAE
Rub-ons: DCWV

you inspire me
Patterned Paper: Scenic Route
Ribbon: May Arts
Flowers: Prima, Michaels
Brads: MM
Rub-ons: MM
Stickers: Sonnetts
Woven Tag: Scrapworks
Chalk: Colorbox

star envelope card
Cardstock: DCWV
Patterned Paper: DCWV
Brads: JAE
Bookplate: JAE

happy birthday coaster card
Patterned Paper: SEI, DCWV
Coasters: SEI
Ribbon: SEI
Brads: SEI
Diecuts: DCWV
Stickers: SEI
Font: 2Peas Flea Market

card organizer
Cardstock: DCWV
Patterned Paper: DCWV
Ribbon: Offray
Puzzle Piece: JAE
Rub-on: DCWV
Metal Letter: DCWV
Word Stick Pin: JAE
Washer Words: JAE

monogram card
Cardstock: DCWV
Patterned Paper: DCWV
Card: DCWV
Ribbon: Offray, AC
Rub-on: JAE

get well soon
Cardstock: DCWV
Patterned Paper: DCWV
Card: DCWV
Ribbon: DCWV
Buttons: DCWV
Brads: JAE, DCWV
Alphabet Stickers: DCWV
Page Pebble: JAE

get well
Cardstock: DCWV
Patterned Paper: DCWV
Card: DCWV
Ribbon: AC, Offray
Metal Tag: JAE
Brad: DCWV
Page Pebble: JAE

happy thanksgiving 2day
Cardstock: DCWV
Patterned Paper: DCWV
Card: DCWV
Ribbon: DCWV
Brads: DCWV
Rub-ons: DCWV
Alphabet Stickers: DCWV
Alphabet Conchos: JAE
Acrylic Word: JAE
Cork Letter: JAE

monogram birthday card
Cardstock: DCWV
Patterned Paper: DCWV
Metal Circle Clip: JAE
Ribbon: DCWV
Brads: DCWV
Cork Letters: CI
Rub-ons: DCWV, JAE
Word Stickers: DCWV

relax card
Cardstock: DCWV
Printed Card: DCWV
Sticker: DCWV
Rub-on: MM
Brads: JAE

happy birthday papa
Cardstock: DCWV
Patterned Paper: DCWV
Card: DCWV
Rub-ons: DCWV, MM
Ribbon: DCWV
Cork Letter: CI
Brads: DCWV
Bookplate: JAE

i love u valentine's tag
Patterned Paper: Foofala, 7 Gypsies, BZ
Chipboard Letter: HS
Photo Holder: 7 Gypsies
Brads: SEI
Lace: JA
Stamps: Purple Onion
Ink: Stampin' Up

friend thank you card
Cardstock: DCWV
Patterned Paper: BG
Card: DCWV
Bookplate: JAE
Metal Embellishment: JAE
Brads: JAE
Alphabet Stickers: JAE
Sticker: JAE

bonjour Card
Card: DCWV
Puzzle Pieces: JAE
Embossing Powder: JAE
Stamps: Technique Tuesday
Ink: JAE, Ranger
Rub-ons: HS
Ribbon: Fibers by the Yard
Metal Charm: Jewelry Connection

liz
Card: DCWV
Cardstock: DCWV
Patterned Paper: DCWV
Ribbon: DCWV
Brads: JAE
Metallic Letters: DCWV

hi card
Card: DCWV
Ribbon: DCWV, AC
Puzzle Piece: JAE

all boy card
Cardstock: DCWV
Patterned Paper: Memories in the Making
Sticker: DCWV
Metal Charms: Memories in the Making
Ribbon: AC, Offray

you hold the key to my heart
Cardstock: DCWV
Card: DCWV
Rub-on: DCWV
Stamps: Hero Arts
Ribbon: AC, DCWV
Alphabet Stickers: JAE
Brad: JAE

it's your day card
Cardstock: DCWV
Metal Tag: JAE
Diecuts: JAE

Home Décor

be frame
Patterned Paper: Daisy D's, Mustard Moon
Ribbon: Maya Road
Ink: Ranger
Canvas: Canvas Concepts

thank heaven for little girls
Patterned Paper: Over the Moon Press
Rub-on: Over the Moon Press
Wood Flower: Over the Moon Press
Sticker: JAE
Ink: Fiberscraps

ava wood board
Tile Board: Provo Craft
Bookplates: JAE
Eyelet Words: JAE
Brad Words: JAE
Brads: JAE
Chipboard Letter: MM
Heart Clip: MM
Safety Pin: MM
Charms: MM
Rub-ons: Scrapworks
Square Clip: Scrapworks
Transparency: Daisy D's
Tags: BG
Paint: Anita's
Ribbon: Offray
Acrylic Dots: KI Memories

photo cubes
Patterned Paper: CB
Wooden Blocks: JA
Tacks: CB
Ribbon: CB
Metal Tags: JAE

altered summer frames
Cardstock: DCWV
Paint: MM
Rub-ons: MM

mosaic clock
Cardstock: DCWV
Paint: MM, Delta
Clock Hands: Walnut Hollow

panama city tin hanger
Acrylic Words: JAE
Stickers: Pebbles Inc.
Glaze: Judekins

grow shadow box
Cardstock: DCWV
Rub-ons: MM
key holder
Patterned Paper: DCWV
Rack: Walnut Hollow
Paint: Plaid
Ribbon: JA
Metal Alphabet Lettering: JAE
Vintage Key: JAE
Flowers: MM
3-D Stickers: JAE
Paint; MM
Shadow Box: Provo Craft

key holder
Pattern Paper: DCWV
Rack: Walnut Hollow
Paint: Plaid
Ribbon: Joann's
Metal Alphabet Lettering: JAE
Vintage Key: JAE
Flowers: MM

chair
Patterned Paper: DCWV

calendar
Cardstock: DCWV
Printed Paper: DCWV
Rub-ons: DCWV, JAE
Brad: DCWV
Acrylic Token: Doodlebug

glam girl wall décor
Patterned Paper: DCWV
Ribbon: DCWV
Buttons: JAE
Brads: JAE
Flowers: MM

disney frame
Patterned Paper: DCWV
Frame: JA
Brads: JAE
Ribbon: Fibers by the Yard
Sequin Trim: Styleability
Word Embellishments: JAE
Metal Tag: EK Success
Disney Clip: EK Success
Ink: JA
Paint: MM

night light
Patterned Paper: DCWV
Ribbon: JA
Rick Rack: Wrights
Buttons: CB
Night Light: Hollywood Lights

baby boy light switch
Patterned Paper: DCWV
Ribbon: JAE
Alphabet Concho: JAE
Light Switch: Darice
Ink: Ranger
Paint: Plaid

clock
Patterned Paper: DCWV
Ribbon: JA
Clock Hands: Walnut Hollow
Paint: Plaid
Brads: JAE
Flower: JA

patchwork magnet board
Cardstock: DCWV
Patterned Paper: DCWV
Rub-on: JAE
Ribbon: DCWV, Offray
Circle Clip: JAE
Metal Frame: JAE
Metal Embellishments: JAE
Brads: DCWV
Flowers: Prima
Metal Saying: JAE

towel holder
Patterned Paper: DCWV
Vellum Quote: JAE
Paint: Americana
Rhinestones: JAE

family vacation fund
Patterned Paper: DCWV
Acrylic Letter: JAE
Metal Embellishments: JAE
Rub-ons: DCWV
Ribbon: DCWV
Metal Letters: JAE

tissue box
Patterned Paper: DCWV
Box: www.popuppaper.com

breakfast tray
Cardstock: DCWV
Patterned Paper: DCWV
Rub-ons: MM, DCWV
Page Pebbles: JAE
Stickers: JAE
Ribbon: AC, DCWV
Fabric Letters; JAE
Paint: MM

waste basket
Patterned Paper: DCWV
Waste Basket: www.popuppaper.com

jewelry box
Cardstock: DCWV
Patterned Paper: DCWV
Gems: JAE
baby pictures frames
Patterned Paper: DCWV
Ribbon: DCWV
Charms: JAE
Rub-on: DCWV

baby picture frames
Pattern Paper: DCWV
Ribbon: DCWV
Charms: JAE
Rub-on: DCWV

riley's boat
Patterned Paper: Rusty Pickle,
Ribbon: AC
Metal Letters: JAE
Sea Shells: JA

wood letters
Patterned Paper: K&Company, Craft Etc
Paint: Plaid, MM
Metal Embellishment: JAE
Ribbon: Offray, May Arts, MM, EK Success, Daisy Hill, Home Arts
Stamps: Stampin' Up
Ink: Stampin' Up
Charms: Heidie Grace, Blue Moon
Brads: Paper Studio
Page Pebble: MM
Rub-ons: MM

Heritage

christmas box
Patterned Paper: BG
Ribbon: Offray
Flower: Prima
Vintage Metal Brad: JAE
Buttons: K&Company
Antique Tag: Memories in the Making
Wood Letters: Provo Craft
Crystal Decoupage: Treasure Tape
Jewels: K&Company

heritage journal
Cardstock: DCWV
Patterned Paper: BG, DCWV
Album: DCWV
Ribbon: Offray, DCWV
Metal Embellishment: JAE
Metal Letters: Sticker Studio
Vintage Letters: JAE
Brads: JAE
Stamp: HS

williams sisters
Cardstock: DCWV
Patterned Paper: BG, Scenic Route
Brads: MM
Clip: JAE
Alphabet Stickers: DCWV
Rub-on: JAE
Ribbon: AC
Locket: JAE
Vintage Key: JAE

memories of grandma
Cardstock: BZ
Printed Paper: DCWV
Brad: MM
Ribbon: Offray

what are little girls made of?
Cardstock: DCWV
Patterned Paper: DCWV
Envelope: JAE
Vellum Quote: DCWV
Brads: JAE
Ribbon: Venus Industries, Stampin' Up
Transparency: DCWV
Ink: Ranger

family time heritage notebook
Cardstock: 7 Gypsies
Patterned Paper: 7 Gypsies
Fibers: Eccentricities
Tags: 7 Gypsies, Rebecca Sowers
Stamps: Stampabilities
Snaps: Memories
Stickers: Rebecca Sowers
Alphabet Tags: Rebecca Sowers
Alphabet Conchos: JAE

grandma & grandpa
Patterned Paper: Provo Craft
Fiber: Fibers by the Yard
Diecuts: Sizzix
Brads: JAE
Ink: Ranger, StazOn, Colorbox, Versamark
Vellum Clock: Paperbilities
Stamps: Hampton
Fonts: Flat Brush Wide, Ameretto Condensed

sisters
Cardstock: DCWV
Patterned Paper: DCWV, We R Memory Keepers
Letter Conchos: JAE
Ticker: Kelly Pancini
Ink: Ranger

vintage mini album
Cardstock: BZ
Patterned Paper: Scenic Route, DDDesigns7
Mini Album: MM
Ink: Van Dyke
Stickers: Karen Fosters
Name Plate: JAE
Ribbon: May Arts

heritage shadow box
Patterned Paper: DCWV
Rub-on: DCWV
Vellum Quote: JAE
Rhinestone: JAE
Stick Pins: JA
Chipboard: MM

thanksgiving card
Cardstock: DCWV
Patterned Paper: DCWV
Card: DCWV
Brads: JAE
Sticker: DCWV

pieces of the past
Cardstock: DCWV
Patterned Paper: DCWV
Puzzle Pieces: JAE
Eyelet Charms: JAE
Brads: JAE
Fabric: JA
Ribbon Fibers by the Yard
Ink: Ranger, JAE, Stampin' Up
Paint: MM
Stamps: Hero Arts
Fonts: Americana BT, 2Peas Tiger Tails

school days
Cardstock: DCWV
Patterned Paper: DCWV
Metal Letters: JAE
Metal Tag: JAE
Flowers: Prima
Brads: JAE
Fabric: JA
Ink: Altered Pages, Ranger
Ribbon: Fivers by the Yard
Safety Pin: MM
Jump Rings: Crafts Etc.
Paint: MM

inspire
Patterned Paper: Memories in the Making
Ribbon: Offray
Stickers: Memories in the Making

far away
Patterned Paper: Memories in the Making
Stickers: Memories in the Making

pocket full of memories
Patterned Paper: Memories in the Making
Stickers: Memories in the Making

franklin heritage frame
Patterned Paper: DCWV
Frame: Walnut Hollow
Paint: Plaid
Brads: JAE
Metal Letters: JAE
Ink: Ranger

roots
Cardstock: BZ
Rub-ons: MM, KI, Doodlebug
Stamps: MM, LD, Bonny Mead
Alphabet Stickers: David Walker, Artic Frog
Flowers Memory Makers
Alphabet Concho: JAE
Pebbles: KI

fathers
Patterned Paper: Rusty Pickle
Cork Letters: JAE
Brads: JAE
Ink: StazOn, Ranger
Rub-ons: MM, Gin-X
Stamps: Plaid, Rebecca Sower

vintage card
Cardstock: DCWV
Card: DCWV
Ribbon: Offray, MM
Metal Clips: JAE
Vintage Stickers: DCWV

love canvas
Metal Word: JAE
Sticker: CI
Collage Images: DMD
Stencils: Rusty Pickle
Canvas Word: LD
Clock Numbers: LD
Tissue Paper: LD

party & holiday

girls' night out invitation
Cardstock: DCWV
Stickers: Magic Scraps
Vellum: Zsiage
Font: LD Dainty

"irish luck" blocks
Rub-ons: JAE
Paint: Delta

eggs to dye for
Cardstock: BZ
Patterned Paper: Bo Bunny Press, Provo Craft
Cardstock Stickers: Bo Bunny Press
Paint: MM
Brads: JAE
Font: CK Newsprint
Ink: Stampin' Up

easter tin basket
Patterned Paper: Me & My Big Ideas, CB
Fibers: JAE, Creative Impressions
Mini Clip: JAE
Metal Charm: JAE
Micro Beads: Provo Craft

beach party invitation
Cardstock: DCWV
Patterned Paper: DCWV
Stickers: JAE
Acrylic Shape: JAE

slumber party invitation
Patterned Paper: CB
Flowers: CB, Prima
Key Chain: MM
Tags: Chatter Box
Nails: Chatter Box
Brads: JAE
Font: Arial
aloha invitation
Cardstock; DCWV
Fabric Embellishment: JAE
Tape: HS
Jelly Word: MM
Metal Charm: Target
Photo Corners: HS

aloha card
Cardstock; DCWV
Fabric Embellishment: JAE
Tape: HS
Jelly Word: MM
Metal Charm: Target
Photo Corners: HS

flip into summer
Cardstock: Archiver's
Brads: JAE
Stickers: JAE
Flowers: JA
Ribbon: JA
Ink: Memories
Flip-Flop: Wal-Mart

make a wish
Cardstock: DCWV
Patterned Paper: DCWV
Button: MM
Metal Word: MM
Ribbons, LD, Offray
Paint: Delta
Alphabet Stickers: Bo Bunny
Photo Corners: Canson
Lettering Template: Pagerz Blocky
Fonts: Goudy Stout, Angelina

party favor purse
Patterned Paper: MM
Stickers: JAE
Ribbon: Offray

birthday bash dvd case
Cardstock: DCWV
Patterned Paper: DCWV
Stickers: DCWV
Brads: JAE
Stamps: JAE

Ribbon: DCWV
Metal Letters: DCWV
Number Stickers: JAE
Rub-on: JAE

barbecue tin
Patterned Paper: DCWV
Rub-ons MM
Alphabet Stickers: MM
3-D Stickers: JAE
Ribbon: JA
Paint Can: Home Depot

barbecue menu
Patterned Paper: DCWV
Frame: JA
3-D Stickers: JAE
Brad: MM

proud to be an american
Patterned Paper: Paper Heart Studio (Digital Version)
Font: Vein, One Fell Swoop, My Old Remington

july fourth celebration
Patterned Paper: K&Company
Vellum: Grafix
Vellum Tag: JAE
Snaps: MM
Rub-ons: MM
Frame Stars: MM
Star Brad: Creative Impressions
Star Clips: Creative Impressions
Ribbon: Creative Impressions
Transparency: Home Depot

anniversary party invitation
Cardstock: DCWV, BZ
Patterned Paper: DCWV
Eyelets: JAE
Ribbon: DCWV
Rub-ons: DCWV
Ink: Ranger
Eyelet: JAE

halloween decoration
Patterned Paper: DCWV
Wood: Provo Craft
Cork Letters: JAE
Rub-ons: JAE, DCWV
Safety Pins: JAE
Ribbon: AC, DCWV

he-he halloween invitation
Patterned Paper: DCWV
Ribbon: MM
Brad: JAE

fairy
Patterned Paper: DCWV, Karen Foster, Petals and Possibilities
Ribbon: May Arts, Offray
Alphabet Stickers: AC
Craft Metal: Artcrafts
Vellum: The Paper Company
Font: 2 Peas Jone Hallmark
Ink: Nick Bantok

halloween card & envelope
Cardstock: DCWV
Patterned Papers: DCWV
Box: Self Addressed
Brads: JAE
Eyelets: JAE
Stamps: Close to My Heart
Ribbon: Fibers By the Yard
Jump Ring: Crafts Etc

halloween box
Cardstock: DCWV
Patterned Papers: DCWV
Box: Self Addressed
Brads: JAE
Eyelets: JAE
Stamps: Close to My Heart
Ribbon: Fibers By the Yard
Jump Ring: Crafts Etc

autumn
Patterned Paper: DCWV
Ribbon: Offray
Stencil: Autumn Leaves
Tags: Avery
Raffia: JA
Acrylic Words: JAE
Rub-ons: MM
Buttons: Dress It Up
Ink: Stampin' Up
Dimensional Accents: Nostalgiques

remember fall
Patterned Papers: CB, K&Company
Stickers: CB
Ribbon: MM
Brads: MM
Eyelets: MM
Buttons: CB
Mesh Paper: Magenta
Transparency: Magic Scraps
Metal Charms: Maude and Millies

thanksgiving place card
Cardstock: DCWV
Embossing Powder: UTEE
Flowers: JA
Raffia: JA
Font: Casablanca Antique

menu
Cardstock: DCWV, Paper Reflections
Embossing Powder: UTEE
Stamp: JA
Brads: JAE
Vellum Quote: DCWV
Flowers: JA
Font: Casablanca Antique

thanksgiving tag
Cardstock: DCWV
Embossing Powder: UTEE
Stamp: JA
Ink: Stampabilities
Brad: JAE
Vellum Quote: DCWV
Flowers: JA

party invitation
Cardstock: DCWV, Paper Reflections
Embossing Powder: UTEE
Stamp: JA
Ink: Stampabilities
Brads: JAE
Vellum Quote: DCWV
Flowers: JA
Raffia: JA
Font: Casablanca Antique

christmas eve
Cardstock: DCWV
Patterned Paper: DCWV
Ribbon: Flair Designs
Label: MM
Charm: MM
Plaque: MM
Button: Jesse James
Metal: Art Emboss
Bellum: The Paper Company
Fonts: Eurostile, Mistral

christmas invitation
Cardstock: DCWV
Paper Edgers: Fiskars
Paper Crimper: Fiskars

camp christmas morning
Cardstock: National Cardstock, DCWV
Patterned Paper: DCWV
Transparencies: Staples
Stickers: DCWV
Ink: Ranger
Epoxy Stickers: Target

things to do before christmas chalkboard
Patterned Paper: DCWV
Alphabet Stickers: DCWV
Ribbon: JAE
Metal Tree: JAE

christmas gift bag
Patterned Paper: Scissor Sisters
Ribbon: Offray, JA
Alphabet Stickers: Kelly Panaci
Rub-ons: JAE
Brads: JAE
Safety Pin: JAE
Ink: Ranger

christmas tree
Patterned Paper: Scissor Sisters
Ribbon: Offray, JAE
Alphabet Stickers: Kelly Panaci
Rub-ons: JAE
Brads: JA
Safety Pin: JAE
Ink: Ranger
Acrylic Words: JAE
Cork Letter: JAE
Vellum Quote: JAE

christmas magnet
Patterned Paper: Scissor Sisters
Ribbon: Offray, JA
Alphabet Stickers: Kelly Panaci
Brads: JAE
Ink: Ranger

christmas stocking invitation
Patterned Paper: Scissor Sisters
Ribbon: Offray, JA
Alphabet Stickers: Kelly Panaci
Brads: JAE
Safety Pin: JAE
Ink: Ranger

resolutions 2005
Cardstock: DCWV
Patterned Paper: DCWV, Rusty Pickle, KI Memories
Buttons: Junkitz
Brads: JAE
Dictionary Words: JAE
Bottle Cap: Lara Cambell
Tags: MM
Alphabet Stickers: Mustard Moon

new year's place cards
Cardstock: DCWV
3-D Stickers: EK Success

new year's party favors
Cardstock: DCWV
3-D Sticker: EK Success

new year's party invitation
Cardstock: DCWV
Ribbon: Offray
3-D Stickers: EK Success

Photo Manipulation

liberty bell
Scrap Kit: Michelle Underwood-4th of July, scrapbook-elements
Font: Persimmon, Zipty Do, Splendid 66

talon
Scrap Kit: Michelle Underwood-Ralphie, scrapbook-bytes/store
Fonts: 1942 report

sweet baby girl
Scrap Kit: Michelle Underwood-Baby girl, scrapbook-bytes/store
Font: Fresh paint

bailey
Scrap Kit: Michelle Underwood-Lullabies, scrapbook-elements
Fonts: Clarissa

lake miniature, ne
Scrap Kit: Amy Jo Smith
Fonts: Colton Grundy, Becks Elegance

friends forever
Cardstock: Paperbilities
Patterned Paper: MM, Carolee's Creations, DCWV
DieCuts: Carolee's Creations
Brads: JAE
Rub-ons: MM
Fonts: Century Gothic

happiness is family
Cardstock: DCWV
Patterned Paper: Zsiage, DCWV
Ribbon: DCWV
Alphabet Stickers: AC Elements
Transparency: Karen Russel
Bookplate: JAE
Rub-ons: MM
Staples: MM

autumn
Cardstock: Provo Craft
Patterned Paper: Gin-X
Leaves: JA
Fabric: JA
Embellishment: Me & My Big Ideas

portrait of love
Patterned Paper: BG
Ribbon: Gingham
Heart Clips: MM
Metal Plaques: MM
Rub-ons: MM
Font: Times New Roman

my champion
Cardstock: BZ
Patterned Paper: Scrappin' Sports and More!
Brads: JAE
Stickers: Destination Scrapbooks
Photo Holders: 7 Gypsies

engagement photo
Cardstock: DCWV
Patterned Paper: DCWV
Brads: JAE

spin
Scrap Kit: Dawn Stocstill & Ali Folendore

kelsie
Cardstock: DCWV
Transparency: Memories in the Making
Metal Letters: JAE
Number Stickers: JAE

one in a million
Cardstock: DCWV
Patterned Paper: DCWV
Photo Holders: JAE
Book Plate: JAE
Brads: JAE
Vellum Quotes: DCWV
Stickers: DCWV, JAE

un tendre calin
Patterned Paper: Junkitz
Alphabet Stickers: BG
Ribbon: May-Art, MM
Photo Holder: MM
Brads: MM
Tab: Melissa France
Ink: Colorbox

with a kiss & a dance
Patterned Paper: DCWV, CB, KI Memories
Fibers: MM
Flower: MM
Sticker: Shotz Thoughtz by Danielle Johnson
Button: JAE
Pin: JAE
Brads: JAE
Tag: Staples

road trip
Cardstock: BZ
Patterned Paper: Reminsce, RI
Stickers: Woodstone, EK Success
Brad: MM
Transparency: Hammermill
Index Label: SEI
Photo Corner: EK Success

tulips
Cardstock: BZ
Patterned Paper: KI Memories
Brads; JAE
Snaps: MM
Rub-ons: MM
Ink: VersaMagic
Chipboard: BZ
Ribbon: KI Memories
Alphabet Stickers: KI Memories

why a scorpio?
Cardstock: BZ
Patterned Paper: AC
Chipboard Letters: HS
Bookplate: HS
Spray Paint: Krylon
Floss: DMC
Photo Holders: JAE
Brads: JAE
Rub-ons: Scrapworks

it's me
Cardstock: BZ
Patterned Paper: Bo-Bunny, AC
Rub-ons: MM
Ink: VanDyke

simply you
Patterned Paper: Zsiage
Specialty Paper: Darice
Alphabet Stickers: Doodlebug
Felt: Kunin
Diecuts: Carolee's
Brads: JAE
Button: JAE

Journaling

i called you mary
Patterned Paper: Sweetwater
Rub-ons: MM
Alphabet Stickers: Gin-X
Font: Poor Richard

life lessons
Cardstock: DCWV, BZ
Patterned paper: DCWV
Ribbon: BZ
Brads: JAE

inspiration journal jar
Patterned Paper: DCWV
Ribbon: Maya Road, May Art, Offray
Metal Tag: JAE
Brads: Junkitz
Metal Word: MM
Alphabet Stickers: Provo Craft

purr sonalities
Cardstock: DCWV
Patterned Paper: DCWV
Library Card: Jest Charming
Blue Letters: Karen Foster
File Folder: Autumn Leaves
Rub-ons JAE

cousins' family journal
Cardstock: BZ
Patterned Paper: DCWV
Transparency Letter: www.alteredpages.com
Alphabet Letters: Doodlebug, American Craft
Ribbon: JA
Brads: JAE
Mini Tag: MM
Book : Target

1st lost Tooth
Patterned Paper: Junkitz, Club Scrap, BG
Rub-ons: MM
Tags: MM
Metal Letters: MM
Hinges: MM
Photo Corners: JAE
Ribbon: Scrapgoods, Hobby Lobby
Number Sticker: AC

family circle journal
Cardstock: DCWV
Patterned Paper: DCWV
Bookplate: JAE
Brads: JAE
Rub-ons: DCWV
Alphabet Stickers: Sticker Studio
Metal Mesh: MM
Ribbon: AC
Paint: MM
Metal Tag: JAE
Stickers: DCWV, Memories in the Making

the gift
Cardstock: BZ
Patterned Paper: Scenic Route
Metal Charm: Icandee
Brads: JAE
Ink: Vandye

things i am thankful four
Cardstock: DCWV
Patterned Paper: DCWV
Ribbon: DCWV
Alphabet Stickers: DCWV, JAE
Rub-ons: DCWV
Fabric Tag: JAE
Brad: JAE
Floss: DMC
Paint: MM
Stamps: MM
Metal Letters: JAE

diagnosis a reader
Cardstock: BZ
Patterned Paper: MM
Ribbon: May Arts
Stamp: MM
Rub-ons: Gin-X
Transparencies: Hammermill
Ink: Ranger

calvin khan
Cardstock: Wausau
Patterned Paper: Rusty Pickle, JAE
Fonts: Century Gothic, Bodini MT, 2Peas Dingbats, Wingdings
crocodile tears
Cardstock: MM
Patterned Paper: KI Memories
Brads: JAE
DieCuts: KI Memories
Zipper: JAE
Ink: VersaMagic
Ribbon: JAE
Metal Clips: Office Max
Metal Letters: Mailbox Letters

crocodile tears
Cardstock: MM
Pattern Paper: KI Memories
Brads: JAE
DieCuts: KI Memories
Zipper: JAE
Ink: VersaMagic
Ribbon: JAE
Metal Clips: Office Max
Metal Letters: Mailbox Letters

cute as a button
Cardstock: BZ
Patterned Paper: Doodle Bug, KI Memories, American Traditional Design
Alphabet Stickers: Doodle Bug, MM
Rub-ons: Dee's Designs, 7 Gypsies, Junkitz, Autumn Leaves, Doodle Bug, Scrapworks
Flowers: Prima
Jewels: HS
Ribbon: May Arts
Buttons: BZ, ISBS Memory Lane
Fonts: 2Peas Cherub, Chesnuts, Empire Dress, Fiori & Flea Market

love notes box
Patterned Paper: DCWV
Stamps: MM
White Letters: JAE

life unscripted
Cardstock: DCWV, BZ
Patterned Paper: BG
Ribbon JAE
Rub-ons: MM, LD, JAE

5 things that make you laugh
Cardstock: BZ
Patterned Paper: DCWV
Rub-ons: K&Company
Fibers: JAE
Brads: JAE
Flowers: Hobby Lobby
Ink: Ranger

why?
Cardstock: Paperbilities, DMD
Alphabet Stickers: Provo Craft, K&Company
Page Pebble: MM
Stamps: Hero Arts
Brads: JAE
Bookplate: JAE
Vellum Tags: JAE, MM
Metal Letters: MM, Provo Craft
Silver Letter Confetti: Hirschberg-Schutz Card Connection
White Letter Beads: Darice
Round Letters: JAE
Silver Letter Beads: Westrim
Fonts: Angelina, Keyleigh, Libby Script, 2Peas Crazy Pooch, 2Peas Squish, 2Peas Gift, 2Peas Billboard, 2Peas Wild Child, Ravie, LD Notepad, LD Diary, Leftovers

what say?
Cardstock: KI Memories
Patterned Paper: KI Memories
Alphabet Stickers: KI Memories
Ribbon: KI Memories

Scrapbooking

me
Patterned Paper: BG
Fibers: JA
Stamps: Stampin' Up
Ink: Ranger, Stamp Craft, Tim Holtz
Fonts: Papyrus

forever
Cardstock: BZ
Patterned Paper: Anna Griffin Inc, Daisy D's
Vellum: The Paper Co.
Ribbon: Bobbin Ribbon
Metal Letter: JAE
Brads: MM
Ink: Tsukineko
Clip: EK Success
Chalk: Inkadinkado
Fonts: Amazone, Lucia Calligraphy

katie
Cardstock: DCWV
Patterned Paper: DCWV
Rub-ons: JAE
Brads: JAE
Number Stickers: JAE
Ribbon: DCWV, JA, AC
Photo Corners: JAE

natural beauty
Patterned Paper: BG
Chipboard Letters: HS
Tag: BG
Rub-ons: MM
Stickers: AC
Brads: JAE
Book Plate: JAE
Flower: JA
Ink: Ranger

chinese garden
Cardstock: BZ
Patterned Paper: Zsaige
Vellum: Zsaige
Brads: MM
Alphabet Brads: JAE
Metal Tags: JAE
Coin: Scrap Arts
Photo Holders: 7 Gypsies
Ink: Colorbox

the streets of paris
Cardstock: DCWV
Patterned Paper: DCWV
Embellishments: JAE
Stamps: Stampabilities, Hero Arts
Embossing Powder: JAE
Embossing Ink: JAE
Ink: JAE, Colorbox
Ribbon : JA
Brads: JAE
Font: Scrap Cursive

london guard
Card Stick: BZ
Patterned Paper: BG
Fibers: JAE
Stamps: MM, CI
Ink: Tim Holtz, Imprintz
Book plate: MM
Eyelets: MM
Brads: MM
Alphabet Stickers: Brenda Walton

hyannisport
Patterned Paper: Paper Company
Vellum: Second Avenue Brothers
Stickers: Soft Spoken Vacation
Ink: Stayz-On
Staples: MM
Metal Squares: Memories
Overlays: Paper House Window Wonders
Vintage Key: JAE
Alphabet Stickers: JAE
Leather Frame: JAE

a winning hand
Cardstock: DCWV
Patterned Paper: Mustard Moon
Ribbon: JA
Rub-ons: MM
Flower: JA
Bottle Cap: Mustard Moon
Brad: MM

sole mates
Cardstock: DCWV
Patterned Paper: Urban Lily
Metallic Tag: JAE
Ribbon: JAE
Rub-ons: MM
Letters: LD

honoring those that served
Patterned Paper: Deluxe Designs
Alphabet Tags: JAE
Transparency: Apollo
Brads; Close to My Heart
Fonts: Calligraph421 BT, Bookman Old Style

drew
Cardstock: DCWV
Brads: JAE
Acrylic Word: JAE
Rub-ons: JAE

got wheels?
Cardstock: DCWV, BZ
Patterned Paper: DCWV
Brads: JAE
Ink: Clearsnap
Fonts: Stamp Act, Tangerine

addict
Patterned Paper: DCWV, Marcella by Kay
DieCuts: Sizzix

a grand obsession
Cardstock: DCWV, BZ
Patterned Paper: KI Memories
Ribbon: AC, Offray
DieCuts: KI Memories
Brads: JAE
Ink: StazOn
Fonts: A Grand, Crazy Crazy
Rub-ons: MM
Staples: MM
Flowers: Ck Ok

major intensity
Patterned Paper: Junkitz
Metal Letters: JAE
Rub-ons: MM
Metal Fasteners: Little Black Dress Designs
Dog Tag: Clare Ultimo
Font: Marydale

the last tailgate
Cardstock: BZ, DCWV
Brads: JAE
Alphabet Stickers: SEI, Hero Arts
Rub-ons: Doodlebug
Ink: StazOn, Tsukineko

my hero
Patterned Paper: KI Memories, 7 Gypsies, K&Company, Me & My Big Ideas
Vellum Quote: DCWV
Snaps: MM
Alphabet Stickers: Wordsworth
Index Tab: 7 Gypsies
Font: Antique Type

volleyball
Cardstock: BZ
Patterned Papers: Zsiage
Transparency: Karen Foster
Paint: MM
Ribbon: MM
Stickers: MM, Memories complete
Photo Holders: 7Gypsies
Brads: JAE

souvenirs d'une vie
Patterned Paper: BG
Rub-ons: Bobarbo, MM
Mini-Book: MM
Brads: JAE
Alphabet Stickers: CB, American Craft
Envelope: Rebecca Sower

you are my everything
Cardstock: DCWV
Patterned Paper: CB
Brads: JAE
Metal Word Plaque: JAE
Rub-ons: DCWV, Autumn Leaves, Arctic Frog, MM
Ribbon: BZ, May Arts, LD, MM
Ink: Ranger

college bound
Cardstock: DCWV
Patterned Paper: DCWV
Metal Key: JAE
Ribbon: DCWV
Metal Tag: JAE
Rub-ons: DCWV

now & then
Cardstock: DCWV
Patterned Paper: BG, Scenic Route
Alphabet Stickers: DCWV, Scenic Route
Ribbon: Offray
Vintage Metal Embellishments: K&Company
Brads: JAE

you
Patterned Paper: Autumn Leaves
Stickers: Autumn Leaves
Circle Letters: Rusty Pickle
Ribbon: Scrapaddict.com
Chipboard Letters: HS
Brads: JAE
Ink: Ranger
Transparencies: Autumn Leaves
Fonts: Angelica, Adorable, Artistamp

love always
Patterned Paper: Over the Moon Press
Word Brads: JAE
Metal Tags: JAE
Transparency: Apollo

new beginnings
Cardstock: DCWV
Patterned Paper: Zsiage
Tag: JAE
Ribbon: Offray
Rub-ons: MM
Letter Buttons: JAE
Fonts: Franklin Gothic Demi

about the author

Nancy M. Hill began designing scrapbook pages nearly 35 years ago, and wishes she could retire and scrapbook full-time. Before founding DieCuts With a View and The Scrapbook Institute, she was a college professor and administrator with a Ph. D in business and information systems. She has consulted both nationally and internationally in the corporate and private sector as a marketing and institutional researcher and strategic planner. She is a Board Certified Genealogist and prolific writer with more than 200 publications to her credit. She and her husband, Mike, are fortunate to live close to and work professionally with their nine children and seven grandchildren.